POWER MIND

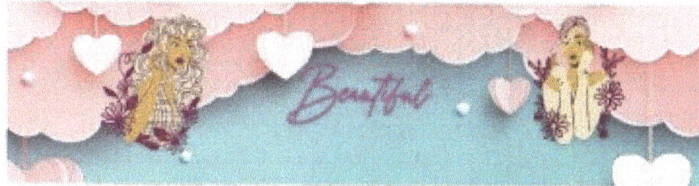

Subconscious Secrets HOW TO PROTECT YOUR HAPPINESS

Los Angeles California

Printed in the United States of America

Library of Congress Control Number 2021940678

First Printing, 2021

ISBN: 978-1-60361-003-2
ISBN-13 978-1-60361-003-2

The Twelve Questions

When You see
ink wells PLEASE use this space to
take the time to Journal
in Here or enjoy the 12 QUESTIONS
Calendar. Remember see the ink well
write there if you want feel free
Plant Ink in those spaces

IN THE BEGINNING
WE WERE A SELF. THAT
SELF KNEW IT WAS A
SPARK OF GOD. PIECES
OF THE ALL THAT IS.
WE MUST KNOW OUR-
SELVES TO ENABLE US TO
FIND YOUR SELF. JOY-

The 12 Questions

DEVELOPED IN MY COACHING PRACTICE

RECIPES FOR WELLNESS

DR. MIA MORGAN WHITE

SUBCONSCIOUS BARRIERS GONE

WAYS TO GET TO KNOW YOU

12 QUESTIONS

these grids are to show allotted times. Time to think, to
partner, to discuss and respond. Give and get answers

Self Time	Express Time	Hypnosis	Balance
5 MIN	20 MIN	35 MIN	1600

ingredients that surfaced

Subconscious exercises

Please remember these are subconscious journeys.
Questions created for my clients at $200 to 500 PER
Session. To access the subconscious. Relax and have
fun answering because you can't guess the right
answer - because I am never asking you what you
think, I am asking strange questions in a way to fix
what you asked me to fix. Need fixed. Practitioners
Never tell your clients the behind the scenes programming (that it is so they can stay relaxed). this is
not a question of right and wrong but of being you.

results PROGRESSIVE DESTRUCTION OF PAINFUL MEMORIES

Dr. Mia Morgan White

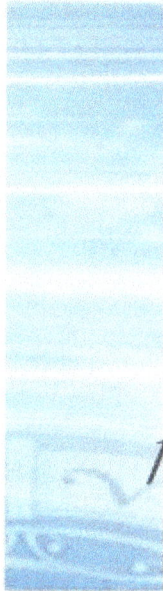

THINK OF PAINTING THE ROSES RED
THE THINGS SOME THINK WHEN THE Y HAVE
POWER OVER YOUR LIFE CIRCUMSTANCE, THAT
INSTEAD OF EMPOWERING YOU ... THEY CAN PLAY
WITH YOUR ENERGY AND LIKE THE SAD LONELY
QUEEN IN ALICE THEY CAN MAKE YOU DO CRAZY
THINGS TO ENSURE YOUR SURVIVAL LIKE
MAKING YOU PAINTING WHITE ROSES RED.

IN every moment we are being programmed by friends,
TV family and others. We don't know this but that's
where our thoughts and behaviors come from... for
something, break bad programming, build a self you
love and figure out what you want to do, without other
people's voices.

12 QuestionsAwaken

MIA MORGAN WHITE

VISIONING MANIFESTED TRIPS

A FUN PROFILING EXERCISE

SIGN UP TO BE A NEW YOU

Previously Viewed

only the good stuff

We are going to do an exercise

directions
this is angel's bridge in rome

1. LEARNED FROM MEDITATION IN ROME LET EVERY BIRTH COUNT. - GROWTH EVERY BREATH BECAME EASY.

2. MEANWHILE, BACK IN THE STATES... AND I KEPT CHANGING ALL POSSIBLE. GROWTH SOMETIMES STARTLING. PAYS YOU.

3. WHEN WE REALIZE MUSIC HAS THE ABILITY TO DIVIDE GENRES AND MAKE SOULS WHOLE. ADJUST THE SPIRIT AND THE SOUL. - DON'T LET STRIFE DIVIDE YOU. KEEP WHOLENESS.

Close your eyes listen to me. If you are reading, record yourself on your phone and listen. Come to a training. Relax and see We have gone to a movie theatre and all the good things in our pasts and futures were filmed as a long reel Every Good Thing. in any order, smallest or chronological order. Take 10 minutes . Watch the Film. save the reel.

ANGELS BRIDGE

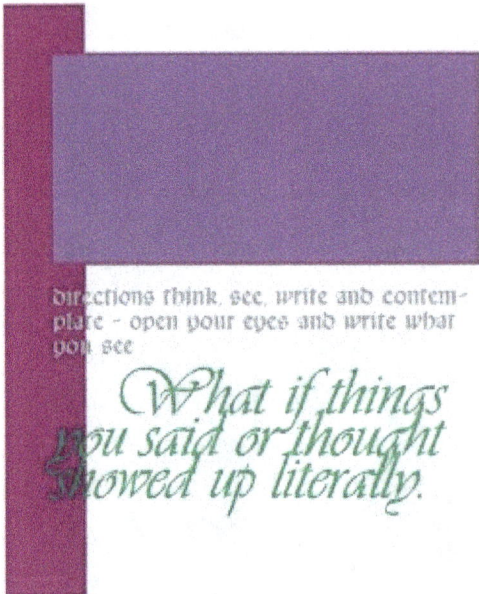

directions think, see, write and contemplate - open your eyes and write what you see

8 Minutes Contempaltion

What if things you said or thought showed up literally.

TEMPLE EGYPT

If you went into time and space what would you go get
places

If You had a Billion dollars what would you do with your day.

Prep time	Answer time	Ready in	Section
07 MIN	22 MIN	02 MIN	11

ingredients

directions
quick write or just contemplate when
doing these questions together.

HEALING ANSWER. THE TRUE ANSWER IS ABOUT WHAT YOU
SHOULD DO FOR A BUSINESS / YOUR PURPOSE LIVING (RE-
VEALED ON SUBCONSCIOUS LEVEL 1QUEST CAN TELL ME 18
THINGS ABOUT YOU THAT ASKING 18 QUESTIONS YOU HAVE
CONTROL OVER WOULD NOT: WHAT YOU WOULD DO IN A DAY

I LEARNED A LOT FROM PEOPLE, WHO SAID: WHAT THEY
WOULD BUY PURCHASE (AS THIS WAS NOT THE QUESTION)
YOU SEE IT'S NOT JUST THE ANSWERS IT IS HOW YOU ANSWER.

SPECIAL NOTE: I TRIED LESS MONEY A MILLION WAS NOT
ENOUGH IN MY EARLY YEARS OF RESEACH TO FREE MOST
PEOPLES MINDS

IS ANSWERED BY

*If You had a Billion dollars
what would you do with your day.*

SUBCONSCIOUS IMPLANT
TRY HEART AND GOAL SEMINAR WORKSHOP
BECAUSE WE DON'T
ALWAYS ADMIT TO OURSELVES OUR TRUE HEART

FOR EXAMPLE THIS IS WHY I WENT TO PARIS.
MY SUBCONSCIOUS DEMANDED IT
FEW PEOPLE SUPPORTED ME
IN GOING, THEY DOWN GRADED THE IDEA OF IT; AND SPOKE
THEIR FEARS FOR THEMSELVES.

NOT MANY PEOPLE SAY, WHAT THEY MEAN
WITHOUT WORRY. MORE PEOPLE SHOULD.

THE CHALLENGING /QUESTIONING OF
OUR NORMS IS THE PART OF THE PATH
TO ENLIGHTENMENT...THE SPACE
NARROWS AS YOU BEGIN TO TAKE
GROWTH MANY OTHERS MAY REJECT IT

Using English, Art, Architecture and History

WE CREATE A SCIENTIFIC JOURNEY

OF THE HUMAN SUBCONSCIOUS. TIME ALLOWS US USING PHILOSOPHY, ART, SCIENCE, CLASSIC LITERATURE BASED ON EDUCATION AND HOW PROGRAMMING BEGAN, AND TRAVEL PHYSICAL AND SOUL; TRAVEL IN MIND OR GO TO A PLACE AND MEDITATE.

I DEVELOPED A SYSTEM OR SEMINARS WHERE YOU HAD TO COME TO THE SEMINAR TO GET THE BOOK. DEALING WITH A STALKER NO ONE WOULD ARREST I CREATED SYSTEMS TO KEEP US ALL GOING. NO MATTER HOW UNFAIR THE WORLD WAS BEING. NO MATTER WHAT HAPPENS DON'T GIVE UP HOPE OR LISTEN TO OPINION OF VOYUERS OF HAPPINESS NEVER HAVING ANY OF IT BUT TRYING TO ENSURE YOU DON'T LIVE YOUR DREAMS. AT THAT TIME I DID A TALK CALLED DON'T GO CRAZY GO TO PARIS.

SEMINAR SETS SOLD ON ETSY.COM

When you picture yourself do you look like you in the mirror

A THEORY ON LOGIC -- DEVELOPED 18 THEORIES : THERE IS ALWAYS MORE HAPPENING THAN MEETS THE EYE: YOU HAVE THE RIGHT TO ENJOY YOUR LIFE.

Peace

You can ask your self or someone can ask
you. Say your answers. Journal or Draw
them

A BILLION DOLLARS

A FANTASY CREATURE

THE MUSICAL YOU

WHO YOU EMPOWER

Mia's Recipe boo
gaining Peace WITH Alternative Behaviors

What is Right, what people think of you or what you think of you?

12 QuestionsAwaken

Mia Morgan White

VISIONING MANIFESTED TRIPS

A FUN PROFILING EXERCISE

SIGN UP TO BE A NEW YOU

MORGAN WHITE

14 YEARS OF CLIENTS

What Super Power Would You Give A VIllain

Answer time	Discovery	Respond in	Serves
10 min	15 min	10 min	3 DAYS

directions
1. ANSWER.
2. ADD TO IT AS NEEDED.
3. LISTEN
4. DO
5. HAVE PERFECT BALANCE

UNDER-
STANDING PRO-
PILING

WHAT WOULD IT BE NOW

Prep time	Response	Determination	Serves
15 min	20 min	25 min	7 years

Use Extra iN a TIME of Crisis your ingredients are:

1 just one genre (gives realistic tool set)

2 look for answer genre not song (is your client listening, were you clear, being a coach means listening)

3 note people who ask other people (tend to get wrong or group answers) that would be cheating

   sheep run in groups LIONS run in packs !

Extra Notes about clients perception:

did they ask how the music would play

did they think of the musics affect on their joy

Because this will become part of their tool box --music that could keep them going

TOOL WILL BE DIFFERENT FOR EVERYONE

If you were stuck on an Island and could only listen to one Genre of Music for Life what would it be

DIRECTIONS

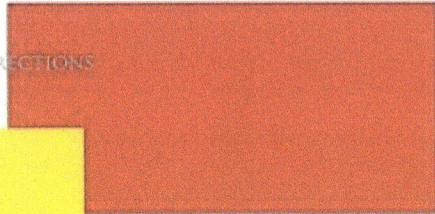

If You had a Billion dollar
would you do with your day.

Prep time	Answer time	Ready in
07 MIN	22 MIN	02 MIN

Ingredients

What things you said or thought or showed up literally.

If you could erase the entire history of two people's deeds who would it be

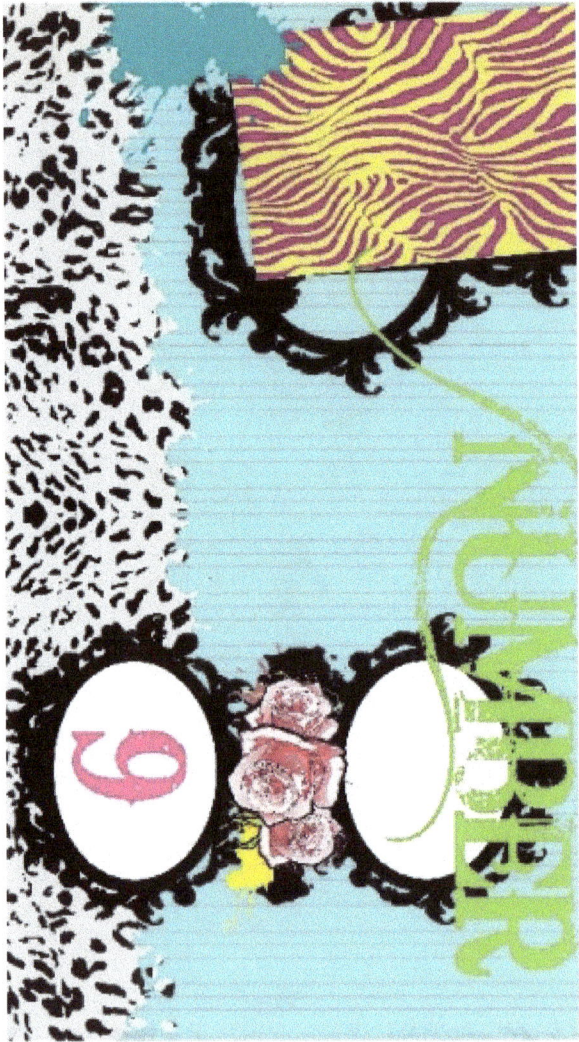

Can You Be A Vegetarian Who Hunts

Prep time	Ask time	Respond in	Serves
5 min	10 min	15 min	18

ingredients

directions

1. EXPLAIN YOUR RESPONSE WITHIN THE RESPOND TIME
2. an ANSWER I WOULD SAY NO BECAUSE_____

you can choose to do anything including stand up against
PAINTING THE ROSES RED
         THE THINGS THEY THINK THEY CAN MAKE YOU
         DO WHILE TRYING TO DRIVE YOU CRAZY

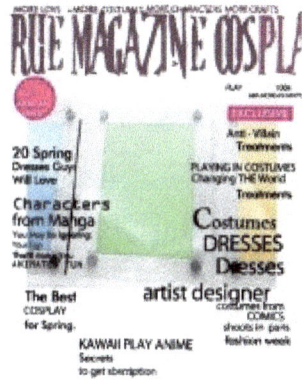

MORE LOVE MORE COSTUMES MORE CHARACTERS MORE CRAFTS

RUE MAGAZINE COSPLAY

20 Spring
Dresses Guys
Will Love

Characters
from Manga

The Best
COSPLAY
for Spring.

KAWAII PLAY ANIME
Secrets
to get sbscription

EXCLUSIVE

Anti - Villain
Treatments

PLAYING IN COSTUMES
Changing THE World

Treatments

Costumes
DRESSES
Dresses

artist designer

costumes from
COMICS
shoots in paris
fashion week

instant
feedback

Habits Of Healthy People

DIRECTIONS

1. Jump In
2. Go Through Doors
3. Don't Stay where you see it's wrong abusive or bad situation to you
4. Who were you - knowing who you are can save your life.
5. Many Tools Gained Here.
6. Offered as a Separate Training.

In Alice who are you

Prep time	Cook time	Ready in	Serves
15 min	20 min	35 min	6

ingredients

Rabbit Holes
Crazy People
Injustice
Liars
Gossips
Corrupt Politicians
Love and Friendship
Growth

Dealing with Unjust situations, compassion fatigue. shows us gossips as Envy Spirits, Spiritual Growth from gifts of Moving Forward. Shows the results of the 7 deadly and the Strength of Self Confidence. Greed, Lust not thinking sloth as in the compared caucus race.

You have the ability to turn people
into anything you want.

Name the People and what would
they be

You Have Unlimited Time to Write Answers to This Question

I Are Who Are You

Does Your Name Suit You.

THE TWELVE QUESTIONS

WRITING MAKES THIS
QUESTION MOST
EFFECTIVE

THE TWELVE QUESTIONS

What is

Prep time	Answer time	Understand it	Serles
5 MIN	10 MIN	18 MIN	8

HOW TO PICK

your favorite question

What Is Your Fantasy Place to Be

Prep time	Bake time	Ready in	Serves
15 MIN	20 MIN	35 MIN	12

instant changing

DID YOU LIMIT YOURSELF BY SPACE AND TIME
PLANNING A NEW YOU
A REAL WORLD OR SCI FI
THESE LIMITS TELL ME A LOT
PARIS WHEN I WENT TO PARIS NO BODY BELIEVED IN ME NOT FOR
ONE OF THE 46 TRIPS. WHAT IF I HADN'T GONE BASED ON SOME-
BODY ELSE'S BELIEF IN MY.
LIST PLACES YOU KNOW YOU COULD LIVE
WERE YOU A PERSON OR OBJECT

Is THERE
Something
Buried Under
The Circus

INSIGHTS
IN YOUR FANTASY WHERE IS YOUR PERFECT
PLACE.

BEAWARE THESE ANSWERS EXPOSES MORE ABOUT
FEELINGS ABOUT WHERE YOU ARE

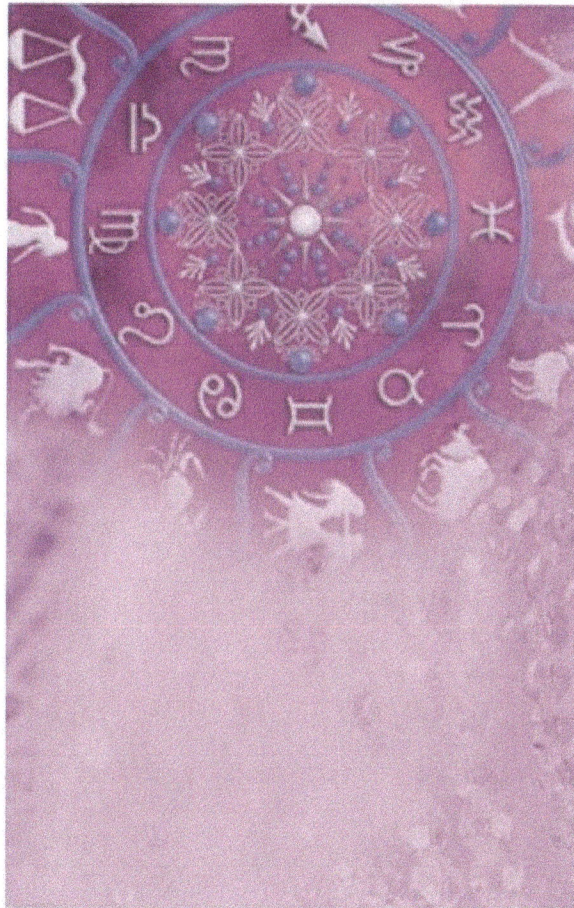
know all the parts
of you

STEP RIGHT UP and see a side-
show
of self

A Few Of My Answers

directions

1. DOUBLE POKER YOU CAN UP THE ANTE
   ANSWER THE QUESTIONS GET DEEPER
   ANSWERS ; OVER TIME YOU WILL GET
   DIFFERENT ANSWERS .

2. EXTRA JOURNEY COME FROM ANSWERING
   MORE FANTASY QUESTIONS. THERE THREE
   TYPES OF QUESTIONS HERE. EXTRA PAGES
   LATER. ABOUT THE SAME AMOUNT OF TIME
   NAME IT.

3. INGREDIENTS SHOW YOU WHAT'S IN YOUR
   SUBCONSCIOUS.

4. HOW TO GET THE TRUEST ANSWER WITH
   THE FREEDOM OF KNOWING YOU CAN'T BE
   WRONG. THE LESS TIME THE BETTER QUES-
   TIONS 1 - 5

5. AN EDUCATIONAL ASSESSMENT TO INTER-
   GRATE INTO YOUR PRACTICE IS AVAILABLE
   AND MAY HELP MORE PEOPLE

Egypt

Health AND

Science

NEXT TITLE HE SAID LET THERE
BE LIGHT AND WE WERE

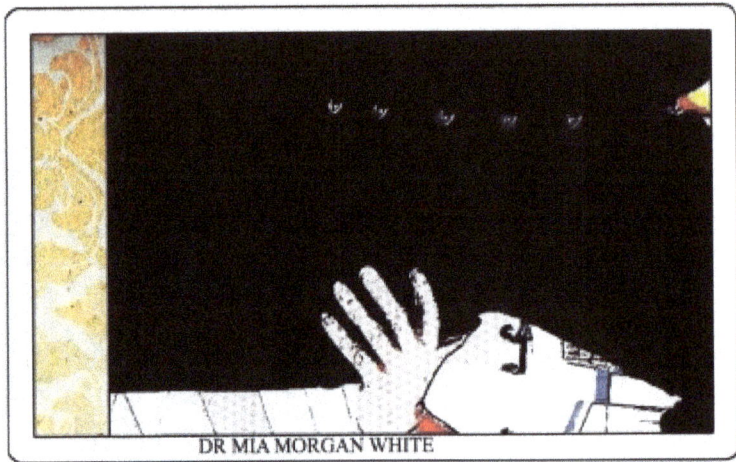

DR MIA MORGAN WHITE

Index

<u>Let's Start With Pulling Pearls</u>
Remove EVERYTHING Connected to a thought you
no longer want.

<u>What is NLP?</u>

<u>The Short Definition</u>

- ✓ Neuro - Brain
- ✓ Linguistic - Language
- ✓ Programming – Behaviour

Referred to as the "Software for the Brain", NLP is a
model for being able to duplicate human excellence
and learn new behaviours at an accelerated pace.

<u>The Long Definition</u>

NLP is a completely unique synthesis of
cybernetics, neurology, and linguistics that offers
you practical methods for rapid personal
improvement.
When you learn NLP, you will discover easy to
follow road maps that lead you to enriched
personal achievement and interpersonal and
professional influence. Literally millions of people
from all walks of life have used NLP principles and
techniques to change their own behaviour patterns
and influence others more effectively.

NLP is not about quick fixes.

In fact, one of the assumptions in the field is that "people are not broken so they do not need to be fixed". Instead, we believe that people have all the resources needed to make any change they choose to. NLP is about uncovering untapped resources within people. You may notice how different this is from today's pop psychology messages that tell people that they are 'damaged' somehow and that they need to recover for a long, long time.
In our culture, there isn't much emphasis placed on purposefully using your brain to direct your life in the way you want it to go. What if you were to deliberately design the inside of your mind and fill it up with wonderful things? This is the premise of NLP: instead of filling up your mind re-living old painful times, why not fill your mind with powerful, supportive thoughts!
NLP is about focusing on who you are, where you are and what you want out of life, where you are going and not so much on how you have arrived where you currently are.

Modelling Excellence - The History of NLP

The field of NLP grew from what its two founders
learned from the mental processes of "exceptional"
people: therapists who created profound changes
in their patients such as renowned family therapist
Virginia Satir, Milton

Erickson MID, (the grandfather of Hypnotherapy
and the man accredited by many with the creation
of clinical Hypnotherapy) and Fritz Perls (the father
of Gestalt therapy), as well as from people who had
recovered from phobias, terminal illness and life's
tragedies, entrepreneurs and top business and
salespeople.
NLP grew from thousands of people who were able
to transform their lives in dramatic and positive
ways. In the early 1970s co-founders Richard
Bandler and John Grinder, at the University Of
Santa Cruz, California, engaged in the study of
people who were able to achieve powerful results.

They asked 'can we determine what processes occur inside the brain that allow these people great successes and can we teach those processes to others so that they too can get the same kind of consistent results?" The answer is decidedly "yes".

They asked a question which leads to excellence. "What is it that these people do inside their head that gets them excellent outcomes?"

Instead of asking what is wrong or at what time in a person's life did something go wrong, they asked "what is right?" They created NLP based on modelling what works – people who got over phobias - not by studying the people who had them. In NLP, we use formulas for success – models and not theories.

A theory is an explanation a person gives as to "why" something is the case. A model, like a model car or steam engine, either works or it doesn't. A model is evaluated by its usefulness whereas a theory is evaluated by its reasonableness. This difference in research orientation and practitioner orientation still exists today.

How to Use Your Brain Intentionally

You and I use our brain and we communicate to others everyday. Neuro Linguistic Programming is the science and art of how we use our brain to communicate with other people and crucially how we communicate with ourselves.

Neuro means our neurology, our nervous systems, and our ability to take in information through our five senses and translate that into usable information within our nervous system.

Linguistic refers to the verbal and nonverbal language we use to communicate with ourselves as well as others. Programming comes from computer terminology. So we can use the human computer between our ears to program in behaviours we want more of and eliminate those behaviours which stand in our way.

NLP is the science of using your brain, your language and your behaviour to get what you want. Basically, it's developing new ways to teach people how to use their brain deliberately and with intent.

It's continued popularity and evolution is testimony to its amazing effectiveness and relative ease of use and speed where change can be effected.

"NLP is an attitude and a methodology that leaves behind a trail of techniques." - Richard Bandler

When people ask in our trainings, "Does NLP 'work'?", we get them to put it to the test, right then and there to see if a particular pattern "works" for them.

POWER MIND IS FOUNDED BY SYSTEMS
CREATED BY DR MIA MORGAN WHITE

What really is NLP?

Sounds like an easy question – it's not, the answers are many. I will give you some typical answers.
Firstly NLP = Neuro Linguistic Programming.

A substantial mouthful which is why the abbreviation is so popular.

The three component parts of the name explain what "It" is.

• Neuro – Brain

• Linguistic – how we talk to others and importantly how we talk to ourselves

13

• Programming – repetition that leads to our behaviours

NLP primarily focuses on studying excellence. Referred to as the "Software for the Brain", NLP is a model for being able to duplicate human excellence and learn new behaviours at an accelerated pace.

NLP is an attitude.

It is an attitude of curiosity and a methodology. NLP is a method for modelling excellence and it leaves a trail of techniques NLP has provided hundreds of techniques for communication and behavioural change.

NLP offers a model for learning how to recognize excellence and how to emulate it.

NLP is a completely unique synthesis of neurology, cybernetics and linguistics that offers you practical methods for rapid personal improvement.

When you learn NLP, you will discover easy to follow directional instructions or maps that will lead you to enriched personal achievement and interpersonal and professional influence.

Literally millions of people from all walks of life have used NLP principles and techniques to change their own behaviour patterns and influence others more effectively.

As you read and use your NLP Training Manual, you will discover the practical nature of NLP. What does that mean? It refers to the emphasis in NLP on modelling, experimenting, and testing in comparison to theory only.

When people ask in training, "Does NLP 'work'?", we get them to put it to the test, right then and there to see if a particular pattern "works" for them.

A common joke within NLP is not to say "how do you do" when you meet someone, but "How do you DO that?"

In the same way NLP practitioners do not need to know why it's a cake, instead they want to know what the ingredients are and the step by step order to make it come out right.

A skilled chef knows that there are many ways to make a cake, that there are different types and has many tools to assist them in making it. Likewise a practitioner approaches processes in the same way by working backwards to the ingredients. Along the way there may even be a secret recipe.

When it comes to creating our reality, it is the sequence or order that we pay attention to things through our senses -- the pictures, sounds and feelings and how those are constructed. As the popular film by the Wachowski brothers, "The Matrix" rightly pointed out, our reality is nothing more than the construct of our mind.

As an example, think of your TV, you have different controls for different functions. You have brightness, colour, black and white, loudness, stereo, surround sound, Dolby. A wide range of functions that you use to control what something looks or sounds like. You can control your brain in exactly the same fashion.

We rely on our senses to gather information about the external world. All of our experiences are a result of what we see, hear, feel, touch, and smell.

In NLP we refer to these senses as the representational system. When we analyze individual skills we find that they function via the development and sequencing of these basic representational systems.

In the NLP model, the five senses do far more than just funnel in information. Each system receives information and then activates memories to produce behaviour. This activity takes place within the realm of the neural connectors of the mind. As we receive information from our senses, our brain codes them in the same manner. For instance, when we receive information visually, our brain codes this information as a picture. The brain

16

codes information received auditory as sounds and words.

We refer to the internal words we form from sounds as auditory digital. "Digital" means that something is either on or off.

Information taken in through our feelings, the brain codes as a feeling or emotion (Kinesthetic).

When you recall information, the brain accesses and expresses the memory in the same manner it stored the information.

Everyone interprets situations through their own perceptions, thereby creating their own reality. Each person may create a different map of the world's Information Input.

We take in information through our senses, and process this information in a way that is unique to each individual on the planet. In doing so, we create software programs that run on automatic until we learn a new program.

Brains rely on our senses to bring them information. We see, hear, touch, taste, and smell things in the world. Once we do this, these sensory experiences are turned into a picture, a sound or a feeling inside our minds.

These pictures, sounds and feelings are then run through a series of filters. These filters are our memories, attitudes and values. These filters then pass the pictures, sounds and feelings onto an even more powerful group: distortion, deletion and generalization, as in the Meta-Model, which you will learn about later.

Submodalities

Within each modality or Rep system, which we will come onto in day 2, are smaller components which are called Submodalities. For example, within the visual modality are Submodalities such as the size of the image, location, brightness and colour.
For the auditory system, there is location of the sound, loudness, and distance from the individual.

The kinesthetic (or feeling) rep system has shape, texture, temperature, location, pressure and duration.

Why is this discovery so critical?

Because it is at the Submodality level that experience is coded, and therefore it is at this level that experience can be changed.

NLP found that by changing the Submodalities without even knowing the content, people could have instant relief from bad feelings. (Try and be depressed by standing straight and tall with a big grin on your face!).

Every moment throughout the day, we have a tremendous amount of information bombarding our senses.

This input is filtered by the central nervous system allowing only a limited amount of information to reach our conscious attention. As an example, when you pour lumpy fluid through a filter, not all of the contents within the fluid are allowed to pass through. In this same way, our filtering mechanism screens sensory input through a set of operations called deletion, distortion and generalization.

Without these neurological filters, we would be overwhelmed by the constant deluge of information.

While these filters serve to protect us, they also explain how is it possible for one person to be excited about public speaking when another person is terrified by it. It all lies in what they do inside their brain and what kinds of directions they have given it.

The wonderful part is that we are limited or enhanced simply by what we happen to be paying attention to or NOT paying attention to at any given moment.

In NLP, we utilize this naturally occurring process to RE-DIRECT the person's brain so that they are paying attention to different things. Each person's internal map of reality will be different. A person's map is an accurate reflection of that person's internal processing, yet it is an inaccurate and incomplete representation of the world.

As you will have found in the last exercise, altering the map (i.e. light, big, small, dark) changes the person's experience in the real world.

Submodalities represent one of the most basic components of the way the brain functions. Identifying and making these distinctions in our internal representations provides specific details for this domain of Submodalities. In a way, they function as the "building blocks" of the representation system.

When an event happens, the event occurs as a fact of history. We cannot change what occurred 'out there' beyond our skin. But once we take cognizance of that fact and represent it inside our heads/nervous systems— then thereafter we respond, not to a fact of history, but to our memory of that event (we respond to our "map" rather than the "territory"). So, while we cannot change external history, we can change our memory of that event (our internal map). When we do, the change takes place at the Submodality level. How we feel about a certain event usually depends upon a few critical Submodalities. Modalities are nothing new.

Visualization and self-talk programs have been around for years. What distinguishes NLP is that the developers discovered that more was involved than just visualizing. What was missing in them were the smaller components they called Submodalities.

Submodalities are the variables within the modalities.

For example:

In visual - is the picture in colour or in black and white?

In auditory - is the sound soft or loud?

In kinesthetic - is the feeling spreading all over or just in one spot?
If a person makes a picture of themselves being motivated- but they make it small, dark and in black and white - they are not likely to become motivated.

On the other hand, if the person makes the same picture bright, colourful, 40 feet tall by 40 feet wide, and add surround sound, they tend to be much more motivated. This is obviously a very simplistic example, but the implications for personal change are immense. In NLP, we call this running your own brain. If there was an owner's manual for your brain, it would be Submodalities.

When you work with Submodalities, you are directly manipulating the structural components of a person's internal experience.

You are working with the level at which experience is coded. By far, it is the most precise technology for altering (re-coding) a person's thinking process. It is important to realize you are not changing behaviours directly. Rather, you are altering states

Submodalities - Desired Outcome

To be able to easily make changes in a client's
internal representations using Submodalities.

Theory: Submodalities are how we encode and give
meaning to our Internal Representations.
Changing the Submodalities can change the
meaning of an Internal Representation.

Techniques Include:

1. Contrastive Analysis: Involves finding the Drivers
(or critical Submodalities) by comparing two
Internal Representations for the Submodality
differences. E.G.: Comparing coffee and tea.

2. Mapping Across: Involves discovering the Drivers
(through Contrastive Analysis) and then changing
the Submodalities of one of the Internal
Representations to the other.
E.G.: Changing the Submodalities of Coffee (liked),
and Tea (disliked) should cause the client to dislike
Ice Cream.

3. Swish Patterns: These involve replacing one
Internal Representation or picture with another.
This energy

directionalizes the series of Internal Representations so that the Desired State is more common.

4. Dissociative Techniques: Involves shifting viewpoint and viewing a specific Internal Representation from a dissociated position. This is frequently used to "take the charge off" a negative emotion, as in the Phobia Model.

5. Perceptual Positions: Involves shifting viewpoint and viewing a specific Internal Representation from one of three different positions. First Position is looking through your own eyes.
Second Position is looking through another person's eyes (usually a significant person in the event). Third Position is observing the entire scene from a dissociated position (say, above the entire event). This is useful as a Dissociative Technique and for incorporating learnings.

Characteristics of Submodalities

As you learnt in the first exercise, Submodalities represent the level at which experience is coded.

Submodalities are homeostatic, which means if one Submodality changes, then the whole system adjusts in some way to the change.

Analogy Distinctions

Some Submodality distinctions can be varied gradually (e.g., from smaller to bigger). Linguistic cues that can help identify analogy characteristics are adjectives with "er" suffixes. In the Meta Model, these are referred to as Comparatives.

Digital Distinctions

Digital Distinctions are either one way or the other. Perceptual position is a digital distinction - an image is either associated or dissociated, which means you are either in the picture or out of the picture. Foreground/background, shape, colour/black & white, still/movement are all examples of digital distinctions.

Synaesthesia or Synergistic Effects

When chaining a component of a Submodality, you can get Synaesthesia or synergistic effects. For Example: When you vary one element – like "proximity" or "distance" – other Submodality distinctions automatically vary. This can happen within one system or between different systems. For example, when you make a picture come closer, size and brightness will often change (one system change). Or, when an image brightens, feelings often intensify (change in a different system). An example of Synaesthesia is often described as "see blood, feel sick". Some linguistic clues: "A bright feeling", "loud colours", "warm tones".

The Critical Submodalities

The difference between two states is typically created by only 3 or 4 Submodality distinctions, called Critical Submodalities.

These Critical Submodalities are the ones you want to use when you are working with someone.

When you are uncovering the Critical Submodalities, remember not to elicit the experiences separately.

Elicit Submodalities from the different experiences simultaneously, and note only the differences. If certain ones are the same (For example: if both pictures are bright), then ignore that distinction. Essentially, the process goes like this: "Think of experience one - now, think of experience two - and notice if there is a difference in the location of the pictures.... the size of the images... the

27

proximity... did you see yourself in one and not in the other .... ?"

How to Elicit Submodalities

The short answer is that you will find your own way, as with all areas of NLP PRACTICE. Some guidance points to help you are;

1. Know your Submodality list. Practice will engage this with your memory

2. Go through it quickly and naturally when working with others.

3. Be conversational - do NOT use jargon

4. Watch your subject while you elicit - stay in touch.

5. Only get the specific information you want.

6. Be disciplined and clean in your language as you ask the elicitation questions.

Why Change Submodalities?

As you will have found in the 1st exercise, changing a person's Submodality's, changes the way a person's perception of their history, their rep System, and changes that way it feels.

Submodality Interventions

Association/Disassociation: For example: See yourself (disassociated) instead of seeing through your own eyes as if you were there (associated).

Change Any One Element: For Example: Within the visual system, you can change the brightness or the size. Within the auditory system, you could vary the location or loudness of the sound.

Delete Elements: Modality Deletions. For Example: If the sound in a movie is unpleasant turn it off Content Deletions. For Example: You can remove the background, people and/or certain objects. Add Elements: Modality Additions. For Example: If a movie doesn't have any sound, add a soundtrack.

29

Content Additions: For Example: In a picture, you can only add content that isn't there. If, when you see yourself doing a certain activity, and you add people, it makes the activity look like more fun, then add the appropriate person or persons.

Contrastive Analysis and Critical Submodalities

Elicit two different states and elicit the Submodalities of each state.

Contrastive Analysis is when you catalogue and contrast the differences in the Submodalities.

The difference between two states is typically created by only 3 or 4 Submodality distinctions, called Critical Submodalities. Once you have determined the Critical Submodalities, you can use them to shift one state into another.

Mapping Across

Shift one state into another by making the configuration of Submodalities the same. For Example: Changing a Limitation State into a Resource State.

Find out what the configuration of Submodalities are for each state and then make the configuration of Submodalities for the "limitation" state the same as the Submodalities of the "Resource" state.

Swish Patterns

The Swish Pattern is often the first Submodality pattern taught in introductory programs and Practitioner training. It is designed both as a starting place to learn about how to use basic Submodalities (size, brightness, location, association and dissociation) and how to set up generative change.
Generative change has a direction built into it, with nothing left to chance or random outcomes. The Swish Pattern is used to create behavioural changes, going from a present undesirable behaviour to future, desired replacement behaviour.

KEYS TO SUCCESSFUL SWISH PATTERNS

• Swish patterns are for the purpose of creating momentum toward a compelling future.
• The Swish Pattern installs choices for a new way of life rather than to change or remove old habits.

Perceptual Positioning

This is a great tool of NLP that enables a person to see a problem from all sides or looking outside the box.

1st Position - Looking at the world from your own point of view. You are completely associated, seeing through your own eyes, hearing through your own ears, feeling what you are feeling.

2nd Position – Consider how the world would look, sound and feel from another person's point of view.

Step into their reality and associate into them, seeing through their eyes and hearing what they are hearing, and feeling what they think they know they're feeling.

3rd Position - As if you are a completely independent observer, someone with no personal involvement, you can watch the world from this position. In third position, you are disassociated in the sense that you are seeing yourself and/or others, but you can be associated into a resourceful state while observing.

We can then learn to take on multiple perceptual positions and even change rapidly between them. Doing so increases our flexibility of consciousness so that we don't get stuck in any one position. This may involve "over-viewing through time"—seeing things as they progress through and over time. None of these positions offers a superior position to the other. Each position has equal importance. The wise communicator knows how to move at will from one position to the other. A person stuck in first position would find himself or herself an egotist. Do you know anyone who lives in first position? A person stuck in second position would live constantly over-influenced by other people's views.

A person stuck in third position would become detached and unfeeling. Others perceive these people as "cold hearted." Indeed, I have found that those who live in third position find themselves as the loners of the world. These people provide society its thinkers and philosophers.

Living life detached permits a person to analyze objectively.

Everyone moves from one position to the other. For most, moving from one position to another flows with everyday life. The ability to move from one to the other, either consciously or unconsciously permits one to act with wisdom and respond appropriately. By moving among the perceptual positions, you will add richness and choice to your conversations. Not only can we get stuck in one position, but we can experience an out-of alignment between these perceptual positions. Problems may also arise from having parts of us react from different perceptual positions. When that happens we end up working against ourselves. Aligning perceptual positions in all rep systems, results in inner congruence and personal power. This pattern also enables us to resolve inner conflict and attain internal alignment.

Practicing NLP

The way you feel and what you experience comes
from where you focus your attention and
determines how you are going to behave.
Successful people know that you must control not
only what you focus on but how you focus.

They have learned to take control of their emotions and run their own brain -- that means taking control of what you are picturing in your mind and how you are picturing it, what you are saying to your Self and how you are saying it. When you get control over these things, this will allow you to determine how you feel.

When you focus, you limit your attention. If you are not focused on success you will miss all the opportunities success brings. In life, we get what we focus on.

Remember this: What you focus on, you will get.

Brains learn quickly to move in directions. Questions direct the mind. They divide experience and lead our attention.

Questions demand an answer. And since it is a question which our brain may not know the answer to yet, it will search to give us an answer.

If, when we ask the question, we include more of what we want in our life; our brain will search to provide us with those things which we included in our question and the answer.

Asking yourself questions is one of the greatest things you can learn for yourself.

Questions set your reality.

Think about it. If I say, "what did you do at the weekend?" Where does your mind go?
It goes to look for an answer.

If I say "how old are you?" You know the answer (though you may have to retrieve it). If I say, "what did you do last summer?", "What is your occupation?", "Who was your best friend when you were at school?"...

These are all directives to your mind to come up with an answer. Sometimes you won't have the answer right away. Sometimes you may have to ask another question like, "Who was it?" You are sending your mind in a direction. The kinds of things you ask yourself are critical.

If you say "Why am I so stupid?" your brain goes "because when you were a child you didn't listen in class, it was your parents fault."

Or because "you are a slow learner" -- because someone told you that when you were a child.

Or because "you aren't self-disciplined enough", or "you have great potential but you'll never really amount to anything".

Whatever it might be, when you say "why am I like this?" your brain will answer and it will come up with a reason no matter how logical or illogical it is.

The number one thing in our culture, bar none, is that when someone in our culture says "why" someone says "because".
When you say to yourself, "I don't understand this" or "I don't get it" you are reinforcing anything that you do not understand yet. You are making it much tougher on yourself. You are impeding your own learning.

On the other hand, if you say, "I wonder how soon before this begins to make sense? I wonder how quickly before I am going to be delighted in discovering what is new about this? I wonder how soon before I delight and amaze myself?" you begin to send your brain in the direction that is useful for you.

As you ask yourself those questions, your brain may not come up with the quick "because" answer because you are posing a question to yourself that you don't yet know the answer to. Wouldn't it be a lot more fun finding out? Wouldn't it be a lot more interesting to think "I wonder how fantastically talented I can become?

I wonder how I can use language to do things that I never yet before considered possible. I wonder who I am going to find that presents a challenge and I wonder how I am going to delight and amaze myself in overcoming that challenge and doing that in ways that I never before thought possible?"

Does that sound like a more useful way to begin looking at the world?

Yes, it is a more useful way, a way that brings you more delight, more pleasure and speeds up the amount of time in which you learn anything?

We have told ourselves a lot of things in our lives. A lot of them aren't even true.

Representational Systems

We rely on our senses to gather information about the external world. Within our bodies we have numerous sense receptors. We have no other way to take in information from the world than through these neurological mechanisms.

All of our experiences, in fact, result as a product of what we see, hear, feel, touch, and smell. Seeing, hearing, feeling, smelling and tasting is how human beings experience the world around them.

These are the five primary sensory modalities by which people encode, organize, store and attach meaning to perceptual input from the day they are born.

In Neuro Linguistic Programming, we call these modalities Representational Systems or Rep Systems.

Input from the five senses is processed in the brain, translated into corresponding internal representations, or maps, that constitute a likeness to the outside world. This means that on the inside we see pictures, hear sounds and have feelings. We can also remember tastes and smells.

What is most important to keep in mind is that our perceptions and "reality" differ greatly because of our filters, deletion, distortion and generalization.

This means that the map and the real world are not the same while most people act as if it is.

When we analyze individual skills we find that they function via the development and sequencing of these basic rep systems. All of our experiences result as a product of what we see, hear, feel, touch and smell.

Each system receives information and then activates memories to produce behaviour. This activity takes place within the realm of the neural connectors of the mind. As we receive information from our senses, our brain codes them in the same manner.

For instance, when we receive information visually, our brain codes this information as a picture. The brain codes information received auditory as sounds and words. We refer to the internal words we form from sounds as auditory digital. "Digital" means that something is either on or off. Information taken in through our feelings, the brain codes as a feeling or emotion. When you recall information, the brain accesses and expresses the memory in the same manner it stored the information.

NLP asserts that the descriptions people use to describe an event the primary rep system will come out in their words.

They also provide a literal description of what a person does inside their head in coding and representing information. This means that the way people represent information using the rep system will come out in their words.

If someone says to you, "I see your point," then they may want to inquire about some visual images! To establish rapport and communicate with that person, we must paint them a picture of our meaning. Trigger and use that visual bias that they have indicated to us.

If somebody says, "I just don't feel right about this," they want some kinesthetic representations.

By giving people back their words (using their own language), we "speak their language" and they think of us as one of them. And people tend to like people who think and act like them. Knowing the primary representation system of others thus becomes an extremely important piece for effectively communicating with them.

These are the first steps in making you a communication master; you will soon be able to tailor your own style to match that of anyone else's thus almost guaranteeing a state of rapport with them.

You do not of course need to have a questionnaire to hand to identify an individual's preferred system.

We identify this by looking at their use of language, specifically something known in NLP as predicates. Listen to the specific predicates or process words (primarily verbs, adjectives and adverbs) that a person uses, we can discover that person's primary rep system.

These predicates thus become language cues (linguistic markers) of the person's internal processing (rep systems).

There is no easier way to gain solid rapport with another than by matching predicates.

Doing so, you verbally mirror the individual's way of thinking when you reflect back their primary rep system predicates.

By matching predicates, we exquisitely pace in a graceful and elegant process. After consciously practicing this for a while, you will find yourself unconsciously matching predicates.

Eye Accessing Cues

Beyond predicate awareness, we can utilize other indicators about a person's ongoing representing. We can notice their other accessing cues. Such cues tell us what system people access and when they access a particular modality.

Internal and external processes that people experience correlate with both eye movements and predicates. As these eye movements provide us such information, we can then use it to establish rapport.

Think about some time when you have noticed that people move their eyes while they talk and listen. These eye movements do not occur randomly.

Each movement of the eyes functions to indicate certain neurological processing.

When we consciously manage our lateral eye movements, this can help to stimulate the corresponding portion of our representational brain.

When I look up and to the left, I stimulate that part of my brain that stores pictures from my past (Vr – Visual Recall)

The eye pattern chart is designed to help you with "typical" cues.

This is usual for a right handed person. Left handed people are often reversed and some people naturally, for no apparent reason cue opposite to what you would expect.

As we are all unique, remember this and verify what the individual's patterns are.

As with all things DO NOT make assumptions.

Furthermore some people make much more subtle movements. For them, one has to observe much more closely to detect the different positions. As you watch the eyes, listen closely to the person's predicates.

Their predicates will provide redundant information about their processing/representing. Once you map someone's eye patterns, you will find that they will tend to use the same pattern regularly and consistently.

Sensory Acuity

In NLP we use the concept of sensory acuity for training our ability to see and listen more effectively and consciously in reading non-verbal communications.

Sensory acuity refers to the ability to notice, to monitor, and to make sense of the external cues from other people.

The other person constantly and inevitably sends out unconscious external signals of some of their internal processing and state.

As we develop our own sensory acuity skills, this allows us to "read" those cues. If so much of the communication messages come to us non-verbally, then developing our sensory acuity skills becomes essential to becoming truly an accomplished communicator. Developing our sensory acuity skills enables us to recognize the quality of another's signals in terms of their congruency and incongruency.

46

By developing and using our sensory acuity we make available to ourselves a great deal of the non-verbal aspects of communication. These non-verbal areas of communication comprise the fuller picture of communication. Knowing and using these levels enables us to build and maintain rapport at these levels—levels that usually operate unconsciously for the sender. Sensory acuity of these non-verbal provides us further a set of indicators whereby we can gauge the level, depth, and quality of rapport.

Developing sensory acuity skills requires time and practice. As you allow yourself to believe that you will develop these skills as you continue to practice them on a daily basis, you will find yourself surprised at times at seeing, hearing, and sensing parts/details of the communication process that previously went unnoticed. To do this, "chunk down" the pieces into small enough chunks to work with without feeling overwhelmed.

Shortly, we will introduce you to some new things to watch for in people. We will offer them to you in chunked-down, bite-sized bits. Then, on a daily basis, begin to observe these in those people with whom you come into contact.

What to look for

1. Breathing: A person's breathing patterns tell a great deal about them. A change in breathing usually indicates a change in internal state. As you begin to observe the variety in people's breathing, notice where they breathe. Do they breathe in their chest or from their stomach? Calibrating a person means that you can recognize certain states in an individual by their non-verbal signals.

Sometimes it becomes difficult to see their breathing because of heavy clothing or shallow breathing. Also, staring at the chest of some people may get you in trouble. So watch the tops of their shoulders. Usually, you can pick up their breathing patterns by watching their shoulders move. This also works well for it allows you to observe their face as well. To further strengthen your observational skills of breathing, turn the sound down on your TV set and observe the breathing of the actors. As you develop this skill, begin to watch the pulse rate of people. You do this by observing their heart beat on the carotid artery in the neck or observing the pulse rate on the temple.

2. Colour Changes: At first this may seem impossible.

However, if you begin to recognize the extent to which you already have expertise in this, then you can become aware of how your unconscious mind already picks up on these colour changes. You can then bring this skill into conscious awareness as you practice awareness of a few things.

First, think in terms of contrast. This will help you notice colour changes. Notice that a person's face does not have just one colour. Faces have areas of pink, cream, brown, grey, green, blue, lavender and yellow. These colours constantly change as a person talks. Facial colours also tend to reflect the internal state of the person.

For instance, detect the differences between the colours under the eye with the colour of the upper cheek.
Secondly, notice how these colours change as the person changes subjects. Often I will change the subject matter in order to have the person reflect an opposite emotion. This will allow me to calibrate the person's response to different feeling states.

3. Minute Muscle Changes: As the colour of the face changes to reflect internal states, so do the muscles of the face change.

The facial muscles change as to tension and relaxation to reflect internal states. Watch specifically the small muscles around the mouth, at the jaw line and at the outer corners of the eyes.

Often when people feel tense, the forehead will tense and the muscles around the eyes will crease.

49

The phrase "tension headache" speaks literally about the process. Anticipate these changes to function in an idiosyncratic way. Each person will respond in his own way to his own internal state. By listening to what the person says and observing his unconscious body signals, you can calibrate what each muscle tone means in that person's system.

As your skills develop, you will become proficient at observing muscular tension and relaxation in other parts of the body.

4. Lower Lip Changes: We doubt that anyone consciously controls the shape of their lower lip.

Indeed, we would probably find it impossible to control the lower lip consciously anyway! Given this, our communication partner will give us some direct unconscious signals if we observe their lower lip. As you begin to observe someone's lower lip, take care that you don't get into trouble! Just notice the changes in size, colour, shape, edges, texture, movement, stretching and tumescence (swelling or filling). Do not attempt to interpret. Only as you have begun to notice distinct changes, and then begin to calibrate as to the internal state the changes indicate.

Calibration becomes possible as we make mental photographs of what each state indicates for a given person. Then we take that picture and compare it with what we see in the other person and whether or not we see the same or different state we are calibrating to.

5. Voice Sounds/Tones: Obviously, voice tone plays a significant role in communication.

Learning to hear the sound quality of a person's voice represents a skill essential in becoming an excellent communicator. Again, changes in a person's voice signify internal state changes. Begin by listening for changes in volume, pitch, rhythm, tempo, clarity, and resonance.

A good way to do this, again, involves listening to the radio or TV. In this way you do not have to worry about the content. Begin to detect the shifts in tonality, pitch, etc. Each of these changes reflects a different internal state on the part of the individual. Once you develop adeptness at this, you will notice just how much more attuned you have become to truly listening, understanding, and entering into another's world. As your acuity develops, start connecting voice shifts with breathing patterns, muscle movements, lower lip configuration and colour changes.

Remember, to chunk this down into learnable bites. As your skills develop in one area, move on to the next. With time it will unconsciously come together. The secret to this involves: practice, practice, practice.

Building Rapport

Matching and Mirroring

We gain rapport with people by acting like them
through a process called matching and mirroring.

When people look, sound, act, and move like each
other, they tend to like each other. What elements
can we match and mirror?

We can match and mirror another's physiology,
voice, posture, gesturing, facial expression,
blinking, words, tilt of the head, etc.

When a person with whom you desire rapport tilts their head, do the same. If they tilt their head to the left, tilt your head to the right. In this way you mirror them exactly as you sit across from them.

Their left corresponds to your right. Notice the curvature of their spine and align yourself with their posture. When they talk, take note of their gestures. As you respond, use the corresponding gestures.
Give them back their gestures as you respond. But do not match their gestures while they talk otherwise your matching might not occur outside of their conscious awareness!

You may wonder, "Won't the person notice my mirroring? How should I respond if they accuse me of mimicking them?"

Not surprisingly, this happens. So match and mirror people discreetly. You can delay your matching and mirroring by a few seconds. If they shift, wait a few seconds and then match their shift.

You may also use crossover mirroring. Crossover mirroring refers to mirroring a portion of a person's physiology with a different portion of your. If they move their leg, you can move your arm.

You may match a person's breathing by moving your finger up and down at the same rate as their breathing.

Such discretion will keep their conscious minds from becoming aware of your mirroring them. You can also match facial expressions and blinking. You can match the tension in facial muscles.

Note their lower lip and shape your lower lip to mirror their lower lip. Take note of the rate of their eyes blinking and match with your eyes.

An excellent way to gain deep rapport involves matching someone's breathing. When someone talks, they breathe out. Match them by breathing out while they speak. When they take a breath, take a breath as well. When you speak to them, talk while they breathe out and inhale with them. If you have a difficult time observing someone's breathing patterns, notice the tops of their shoulders. The rise and fall of their shoulders will reveal their breathing pattern.
A great portion of communication occurs through the auditory tonal channel.

As you match someone's voice tone you have another marvellous avenue for gaining rapport.

Match the tone, speed, quality, and volume of their voice. If someone has a soft voice, then match their softness. Should they speak rapidly, then you match their voice with the same speed.

If they speak loudly, you speak loudly. Matching someone's voice provides an excellent tool in gaining instant rapport.

Difference Between Matching & Mirroring

In building rapport, we match and mirror physiology, tonality and words.

What differs between these two verbs of matching and mirroring?

The difference lies in degrees.

When you mirror someone, you take on and "become" their mirror image. If they have crossed their right leg over their left leg, you cross your left leg over your right leg.

Since you stand opposite them when you face them, you mirror them by crossing opposite legs.

In mirroring their words, you give back to them their exact words. If you match someone's words, you do not give back to them their precise words. You rather seek to match their general rep system.

If they say, "I don't see what you are saying," you match by responding, "Sure, let me show you what

I mean." A mirroring response would go, "I know you don't see what I am saying." In matching physiology with someone who has crossed right leg over left leg, you would match them if you crossed your right leg over your left leg. This works similarly to cross-over mirroring. In mirroring we do precisely as the person does; in matching, we match more generally.

Mismatching

When you do not want to build rapport with another, you can use mismatching.

This works in the completely opposite way to matching another person.

Why learn Rapport

Whether you're a salesperson, a teacher or even a carpenter, no matter what you do, the ability to develop and maintain rapport with the large numbers of people of varying backgrounds will allow you to get what you want.

The basis of rapport is that when people are like each other, they like each other. When people are not like each other, they don't like each other. When you like someone, you are willing to assist them. 38% of all communication is tone of voice, and 55% is physiology. So, most communication is outside of our conscious awareness. A tremendous opportunity exists for communication outside of normal channels, and that's what rapport is all about.

Physical mirroring of the individual's physiology is a key skill in building rapport.

Actually physically copying their posture, facial expressions, hand gestures and movements, and their eye blinking will cause their body/mind connection to believe that you are like them. It's undeniable to the nervous system.

So what if you match their voice?

The tone, tempo, timbre (quality of the voice), and the volume.

You can also match their key words. Perhaps they often say, "Like." You can use it in a sentence several times. Say it back to them.

Also you can match their breathing. You can pace someone's breathing by breathing at exactly the same rate as they do (matching the in and out breath). By matching their breathing, by pacing their breathing, you can then begin to lead them out of the representational system they're in, into another one.

You can match the size of the pieces of information (chunk size or level of abstraction) they deal with. If someone usually deals in the big picture, they will probably be bored with the details. On the other hand, someone who is into details will find that there's not enough information to deal with, if you only give them the big picture. So make sure that you are matching the content chunks that the person deals with.

Also match their common experiences.

This is what's usually called rapport.

When people first meet, often their early relationship is about matching common experiences, common interests, background, and beliefs and values and their ideologies and common associations.

The most effective methods are Matching or Mirroring the predicates, the vocal qualities and nonverbal body language, the chunk size (whether the person likes the big picture or the details) and values (what's important to the person). Detect and match in your own language the primary predicates of the other person. Match eye accessing cues.

When we speak, we give clues about how we think. Because we choose our words unconsciously, they give an accurate description of how we make sense of the world we live in. We use words that describe how we process the information we take in through our five senses. We talk about what we see, hear, feel, smell and taste in the world as well as what is going on inside our heads.

The NLP Communicator learns to listen for these predicates (buzz words) and matches them back to the person he is communicating with.

If someone is painting a picture using visual words, when speaking to that person, the NLP'er paints them a picture as well. If they are talking about how things sound or feel to them, the best communicator speaks in similar terms.

The listener receives the message that the NLP expert hears and understands them. This is a major step in increasing the degree of Rapport and understanding between people.

People may use one or two of the sensory systems.

Most tend to use more than one. Follow the sequence they use. If you treat a visual like a kinesthetic person, the visual person simply won't respond. They literally won't "see eye to eye with you". You pay attention and you can do anything else, switch modes to communicate more effectively.

Listen for the tone, tempo, and volume, rate of speech and pauses of the person with whom he is interacting, and as accurately as possible, matches back these elements in subtle ways. For example, if someone speaks slowly, the Expert NLP Communicator slows down the rate of his speech, if the person talks loudly, then the expert adjusts his volume to match that volume

The NLP Communicator matches the other person's body posture, facial expressions, gestures, and breathing rate. Again, as the expert communicator adjusts the features of his/her communication style to match the person with whom /she is relating, an unconscious message is sent to the other person.

That person receives the message "this person is like me." Communication research has heavily identified that we tend to like people who are like ourselves.

Mirroring is to match back the person's behaviour as a mirror image. So that as the person looks at the NLP Communicator, the person sees is a mirror image of himself.

Adjust your body to approximate the other person's posture. Pace any consistent or stylistic use of the body - eye blinks, head nods etc. Match the upper or lower portion of the other person's body. Note the way the other person uses their face, raises their eyebrows, wrinkles their nose, etc.

Match characteristic poses the other person offers with their head and shoulders. With minute movements and timing, match the gesture patterns of the other person. Adjust your own breathing to synchronize with the other person's breath rate and location. (Watch the rise and fall of their shoulders to determine this.) If a person likes the "big picture", the NLP'er presents the "big picture". If the person prefers the details, then this is how the expert alters his/her communication.

You will notice that chunk size preference is generally sequential, or that which the person wants to hear first. Some start off with big picture and move toward filling in the details, while others prefer it reversed. People are unique, remember that and treat them accordingly.

You can match and replicate people's key gestures; these are repetitive gestures that occur usually to emphasize a point and are frequently accompanied by a shift in voice volume.

Replicate their key gestures so that when you make a point you can use their gestures. You are sending that unconscious message that "I am like you" – which means they are more likely to see, hear or feel that your point is important because it is the same way they act when they make important points. And remember "people like people who are like themselves".

Repeat key words and phrases just as you repeat the key gestures. Key words and phrases are repetitive and are given special emphasis by a subtle but noticeable shift in volume or rate increase and are often accompanied by a key gesture. When someone is angry you should increase your rate and volume to match theirs.

Do not match their anger unless you direct it away from them. Be angry with them but not at them. In other words, pace their energy, rhythm and intensity but do not get angry at them.

This works because:

1. You are matching their current on-going experience and sending a message of empathy instead of mismatching by trying to calm them down,
2. They feel you are listening to them and are willing to do what it takes to remedy the situation for and with them.

It is absolutely essential to learn to be flexible in your behaviour, as well as be willing to do so, when you are learning Rapport methods and all other methods in this course.

Learning to become more flexible, to be able to communicate more effectively with a wider range of people requires practice and a willingness to do things that at first may seem strange. It is amazing just how much more effective you will become by taking a little time to practice and implement the methods.

True Art of Communication

1. Determining what you want to occur between parties during the communication interaction.

2. Observing and hearing without bias, becoming flexible enough to alter your behaviour to increase or break Rapport.

3. Having the sensory acuity to recognize whether you are getting closer to or further from what you want to occur and having the flexibility to adjust your behaviour accordingly to get your outcome.

To establish rapport, the process is to match and mirror completely, what the other person is doing. You do need to be subtle when doing matching and mirroring, but typically most people are in a trance when talking anyway.

They're so caught up in what they're going to say next that they are rarely fully aware of what you're doing. And if they do, remember the key to flexible communication and then you can have a good laugh about it.

Calibration

Calibration is one way of testing whether you're in rapport with someone.

Simply, that means you need to develop your sensory acuity to such an extent that you can begin to see people's reactions to your communication.

Watch their eyes, the muscles around the eyes, the lower lip, the colour of the face and hands, the breathing.

These are all indicators of rapport. Practice your sensory acuity, learn the rep systems predicates and become aware of the subtle nuances of communication.

After you've matched and mirrored a person for say, 5 or 10-minutes, you can then begin to lead them and to lead their behaviour. Successful leading is another way you can tell if you're in rapport with someone.

NLP Presuppositions

So what is a presupposition? It's basically an assumption, a guide that if we believe and act as though something is true that we approach things in a different way. Presuppositions are Linguistic Assumptions NLP has many and I aim to make the list below as thorough as I can though I am sure more will be added during the course of your life long learning with NLP so I have left space for you to add additional one's or create some of your own.

1. "The map is not the territory"

2. "People respond according to their internal maps"

3. "Meaning operates context-dependently"

4. "Mind-and-body inevitably and inescapably affects each other"

5. "Individual skills function by developing and sequencing of our representational systems"

6. "We respect each person's model of the world"

7. "Person and behaviour are different phenomena. We are not our behaviour"

8. "Every behaviour has usefulness—all behaviour comes from positive intentions"

9. "We evaluate behaviour & change in terms of context and ecology"

10. "We cannot not communicate"

11. "The way we communicate affects perception & reception"

12. "The meaning of communication lies in the response you get"

13. "The one who sets the frame for the communication controls the action"

14. "There is no failure, only feedback"

15. "The person with the most flexibility exercises the most influence in the system"

16. "Resistance indicates the lack of rapport"

17. "People have the internal resources they need to succeed"

18. "Humans have the ability to experience one-trial learning"

19. "All communication should increase choice"

20. "People make the best choices open to them when they act"

21. "As response-able persons, we can run our own brain and control our results"

Their Meanings

1. The Map is not the territory:

People operate from their personal map of the world. This map is an internal construct made up of pictures, sounds and feelings. We formed this map during our lives accidentally and we have made premature cognitive commitments which shape our present day reality.

Or think of it this way; when in a restaurant ordering food, the menu describes the food and indicates what it may be like based on your own previous experience, it is not the actual food itself. These cognitive commitments form the basis for the programs we run.

NLP is the software for the human mind. Using NLP concepts and principles you can begin to bring your brain under your control and have more of the kinds of feelings and thoughts that you enjoy.

You can learn to train your brain to get it to give you more and more of what you truly want and deserve.
If we don't program our brains, they will run on and on, they do what they were accidentally preprogrammed to do.

If we don't gain control of our own brain, we are subject to those around us who know how to influence us. Therefore it is crucial to learn to program your brain.

What goes on inside our head concerning an event does not comprise the event; it only comprises our perception of that event. Keep in mind that our perceptions and "reality" differ greatly from other peoples because of our filters (deletion, distortion and generalization.)

This means that the map (internal sensory re-representations) and the real world are not the same though most people act as if it is.

2. People respond according to their internal maps:

We respond to the world, not as the world exists but according to our "map" of it. Within our consciousness, we experience these internal "maps" as simply our "thoughts" through our representational system.

Yet "as we so think—so we are." In this way our internal representational "maps" interact with our physiology to produce our states. Then our state drives our behaviour.

We respond according to our internal "map" of the world. So does everybody else. Everybody uses their model of the world to guide their perceptions, thoughts, emotions, and actions.

This includes your spouse, children, friends, parents, authority figures, etc. Before we can expect someone to change their thinking, acting, responding, etc., their internal "map" must change

To assist someone in changing that, we must develop enough flexibility in communicating that we can assist them in shifting their own internal maps.

3. Meaning operates context-dependently:

All words require some context for meaning. In themselves, words contain no meaning.

A statement or an act in one context may mean something entirely different in another context. This is demonstrable easily in daily life, think about a time when you have said something to a loved one and they have responded in an unexpected way.

The meaning they have assigned to what you have said is different from what your intended meaning was. When you tell your parent you love them, think how this differs from how you tell your lover/partner/spouse that you love them.

The context of the statement determines or frames the meaning of the statement.

When a client says, "I am depressed," we don't ask, "What causes your depression?" His answers to that will not help him. It only provides reasons that support the discomfort, pain and depression. An internal problem exists because of its structure. Instead ask, "How do you do that?" This how question enables us to move from the content level of the depression to the process level. Expect confusion.

The client will usually respond, "What do you mean? 'How' do I do that?"

Help the person shift, "Sure. You experience this thing called 'depression', how do you get yourself into such a state? If I took your place for a day, what would I have to do to think and feel as you do?" "What do you do inside your mind-body to create the depression?"

In this way, we search for the process (the Neuro-linguistic process) within the client that enables them to code and then experience depression.

Remember, each person based on their own unique maps will experience depression in a unique way. Once we discover the structure, we lead the client to change the structure. And that changes the experience. Guess what, once you know what you do and how you become depressed you can change it.

4. Mind-and-body affects each other:

The "mind" occurs within the body (the nervous system) and when we inject psycho dynamic drugs into it the "mind" becomes greatly affected. The mind itself is not even a tangible thing. The brain we can locate and identify and break down into component parts, the mind is another construct yet there appears to be little doubt that the "mind" exists in some way.

Likewise, when we inject thoughts, either pleasant or unpleasant, into the "mind", the body becomes affected. The mind-body functions as a holistic whole. The mind-body interaction further explains the "placebo effect." Studies have indicated repeatedly that one's belief about a particular medication tremendously affects the effectiveness of the medication.

Neurotransmitters which were thought to exist in the brain have been discovered by science all throughout the body. This clinically proves (if there was ever any doubt) the mind and body connection.

5. Individual skills function by developing and sequencing of our representational systems:

NLP takes the view that skills arise and function through "the development and sequencing of our representational systems."

A strategy describes the sequencing of rep systems, whereby we can produce a certain outcome intentionally.

A strategy refers to any internal set of experiences which consistently produces a specific outcome. Most of our strategies for living, thinking, interacting, etc., develop at a young age.

Unconsciously we learned that a specific sequence of our rep systems would produce a certain result. From then we generalized that strategy to all occasions calling for that result. You therefore can break down a strategy that does not work well and instead change it to a more productive strategy.

As an example when modelling students with good spelling scores it was identified that their primary rep system was visual. Breaking this down further their actual strategy for spelling could be formulated as a process... A productive spelling strategy goes along the following lines.

First, you hear a word (auditory external), then you make a picture of the word (visual creation) and looking at it you feel good/right about its correct spelling (kinesthetic). Then, to rehearse the spelling, you retrieve your picture of that word (visual recall).

Good spellers usually look up or straight ahead as they internally see the word and have a good feeling of rightness about it. Seeing the word, you can now spell out the word verbally (auditory digital, internal dialogue).

Then with the feeling of familiarity for spelling it correctly (kinesthetic internal), you spell it externally (auditory digital external).

Now this is known it can be taught to students to enable them to spell with greater ease by following the successful spelling strategy.

6. We respect people's models of the world:

If "the 'map' is not the 'territory'," and if everybody operates from their own "map", then everybody processes information in their own unique way.

There is no reality, just our perception of it. It may differ from another person's, it does not make either of them right or wrong – just different.

Recognizing the map/territory difference, we also recognize that people will map reality out in different ways. This enables us to respect their right and responsibility for dealing with the world. We need to maintain communication adaptability to see their world their way.

A hazard for any effective communicator arises at this very point. If we don't respect their "map" even with all the errors and distortions we believe it contains, we create unnecessary conflict and prevent ourselves from communicating effectively.

7. Person and behaviour are different phenomena. We are not our behaviour:

If "the meaning of our communication lies in the response we get" then some of the most important information we can pay attention to involves a person's behaviour. To say this, implies that one's behaviour does not define them. It may express them—their values, style, etc. But it does not identify them.

By realizing that when a person performs a particular behaviour and that this differs from their ultimate identity, then we can expect and hope that in another situation or another time that

74

person may behave differently. That makes behaviour contextual. Provide another context, and the person may behave in a drastically different way.

We make a major mistake in our relationships whenever we equate a person's worth or identity with a particular behaviour.

8. Every behaviour has usefulness. All behaviour comes from positive intentions:

The NLP model starts from the assumption behaviour has a positive intent driving it. Thus, every behaviour has a useful value in some context.

Again, this does not approve of immoral, unethical or damaging behaviour. It rather separates person from behaviour and recognizes that, as "behaviour", there probably exists some context in which behaviour has value.
When we engage in inappropriate behaviour, we seek to accomplish something, something of value, something important—and so we do the best we can with the resources we have. Think of the naughty child....

Why are they behaving that way, what does it give them, attention maybe? Our intent, at the time, involves a positive intent, but gets filtered through limited understandings and maybe outdated ideas,

NLP allows us to renew our focus, our beliefs, and values and change the way we think.

In working with people, we seek first to discover the positive intent behind the behaviour. We assume it exists and go pursuing it. And here shows the wonder of this approach—even if it did not exist previously, by asking about it, pursuing it in the life of a person—they have to create that internal representation to make sense of our words and thereby internally create it within themselves.

9. We evaluate behaviour & change in terms of context & ecology:

As we act, behave, and respond to people and events, this presupposition challenges us to develop awareness of the impact of our actions and to check the ecology of our responses.

In other words, our behaviours do not occur in a vacuum, but in a system of other actions, ideas, feelings, etc.
Accordingly we should take into account the total system (individual, family, co-workers, etc.) and evaluate our behaviour in terms of that context and its usefulness therein. Seeking to make changes in ourselves and others will have systemic implications. Let us evaluate the desired change in such a manner so as to make the change congruent within the person and the system.

When we work with many of the parts within human "personality," each part must also take into account the ecological question about the whole person. "Will this have any negative consequences that I need to consider?" We can also extend ecology to the person's larger relational systems: "Would this change in a congruent way with the other people in this person's life?"

It's really a case of becoming aware of the effect of your actions on the people and things around you and being accountable for those changes. Making sure all areas of your life are congruent with any changes.

10. We cannot not communicate:

Since communication involves the sending of signals to another—even when we attempt not to send a message to another—that comprises "a message" and the indicators or signals of that message will leak out.

Think about that peculiar silence that exists that has a density or weight about it, the heavy silence post argument? Even when we don't put our thoughts, feelings, ideas, beliefs, understandings, decisions into words and express them to another—such internal phenomena get communicated non-verbally in a multitude of ways.

11. The way we communicate affects perception &
reception:

A great portion of communication occurs via
non-verbal means. This indicates that we always
and inevitably not only communicate the
communication more than how we say things (the
non-verbal facets: tone, volume, facial expressions,
breathing, posture, etc.).

Sometimes, however, one of our messages may
refer to another message. Saying, "I love you!"
carries one meaning. Saying it sarcastically
another. Saying it with fingers crossed another.
Saying it in tears—yet another.

The way that we use our signals can tremendously
affect the way people hear, perceive, and receive
us. Many people give more weight to tonality or
physiology or eye contact or some other
non-verbal facet than the linguistic content. Others
reverse that.

This suggests the importance (and power) of
congruency—aligning all of our communication
channels so that they communicate the same
message and don't conflict or contradict each
other. Congruence makes our communicating
believable.

12. The meaning of your communication lies in the
response you get:

Communication refers to the exchange of information. It operates in a system of feedback responses from sender and receiver, not a monologue.

The response of the person with whom we communicate reflects the effectiveness or ineffectiveness of our communication. If they respond to our communication in the manner we desire, we have succeeded. If their response differs from our desired outcome, we can simply send other signals.

This model leads to a non-blaming style. Regardless of your intent in communication, when you measure the effectiveness of your communication with the response you get, you take 100% responsibility for the communication.

The response you get indicates what you communicated to the other person—in spite of what you intended. Take it as feedback and use it.

Responsible communication means that I always have the option to make changes in my communicating until I get my outcome. If I only take partial responsibility for my communication, I will more likely give up trying. What do you want from another when you communicate? Identify your desired outcome for conversing. Taking full responsibility for your communication helps you to order your communication signals until you get the response you desire.

13. The one who sets the frame for the communication controls the action:

We all live within a frame of reference. The frame governs perception, meaning, perception, emotion, behaviour and values.

To live within emotion, behaviour and values.

A frame means to use some paradigm that gives meaning to things. To get out of that frame, or to set a new frame, thereby reframes and invites a whole new world of meaning. Therefore, in relating and communicating—he who sets the frame truly governs the interpersonal field that results.

The power of setting a frame lies, in part, in that whoever sets the frame essentially does so apart from consciousness. Consequently, people lack awareness of it and therefore cannot bring their conscious values to bear upon it. In communication, people frequently set Win/Lose frames or Win/Win frames; Dignity Preserving frames/Dignity Denying frames, etc

14. There is no failure, only feedback:

What would not happen if you receive 'failures' as feedback? This is a powerful presupposition and gives you permission to learn in a truly positive way.

If you communicate with someone and fail to get the response you want, what do you do? You alter your communication—the stimuli that you present until you get the response you want. In this way, you turn failure into feedback.

Living life by this presupposition changes all areas of life, but especially those areas that demand persistence and the wisdom of learning from "what doesn't work." People tend to give up too easily. Many marriages would not end in divorce if the couples considered communication as feedback rather than failure. Thomas Edison's numerous experiments in search for a filament to work in his light bulb illustrates this principle.

When asked, "It must be hard to have failed 10,000 times!" Edison replied, "I didn't have 10,000 failures. I just found 10,000 ways not to make a light bulb."
How many relationships end because people "fail" to get what they want immediately? How much business ceases because people take "failures" as a reason to quit or back off?

Strike the word failure from your vocabulary right now, and instead replace it with feedback and your life immediately will become richer and more exciting.

15. The person with the most flexibility exercises the most influence:

In any system, the one with the most flexibility over their own behaviour exercises more choices and therefore will exercise more influence in the system. Accordingly, the more choices you have in your communication toolbox, the less chance you will get stuck.

For instance, _ should you become angry, you lose flexibility and you also lose control of the processes of communication. We recommend learning to use the NLP toolbox so that you radically increase your choices. Known as the Law of Requisite Variety, this belief as it applies to NLP encourages us to dissociate from our emotions so as to maintain choice in our communicating. We always have choice available, give yourself more choice and you will change your outcomes.

16. Resistance indicates the lack of rapport:

We speak with people one time, get resistance, and never return; and so, we lose the joy and rewards of the relationship we could have had with them, why?

In addition to using that as a trigger for "feeling bad/ we simply lack the skills necessary for working with and overcoming the resistance.

Consider the power of this presupposition about resistance. It shifts responsibility to us—in how we handle it.

Believing this empowers us to re-establish rapport even with the grouchy, the grumpy, the out-of-sorts, the hurting. This belief also enables one to continue communicating even in the face of anger and sarcasm without taking it personally.

It keeps us matching their internal reality by "saying words that agree with their internal model of the world." The NLP model teaches us how we can overcome resistance. We can overcome resistance even with irate people. Rapport moves us into a more harmonious state with another. When two people adopt the "same mind" about something—they enter into rapport.

Detecting resistance from someone signals to us that we have lost rapport. Obviously, establishing and maintaining such rapport plays an essential role in communication.

17. People have the internal resources they need to succeed:

NLP looks upon people as having an inherent ability for coping, and for creating the resourcefulness that they need to attain their definition of success.

The co-founder of NLP Richard Bandler stated, "People work perfectly well, they just run very poor programs (depression, procrastination, defensiveness, etc.) very well!"

As communicators and therapists we seek to assist people in accessing their own resources—in "equipping" them to develop more skill. People only need some help in discovering and accessing their resources.

In saying this, bear in mind that we do not say you have "everything" in place, we say you have all the resources you need to get "everything" in place. As an example, you may need to further your education or to obtain specific training in order for you to have success.

In NLP we say you have the resources necessary in order for you to obtain the education and/or training you need to have your success. You have the "wiring" in your neurology to produce that success. NLP can often direct you into how to tap into it.

18. Humans have the ability to experience one-trial learning:

The human body exists as quite a system. Each of us lives as an amazing bio-electro-chemical information processing unit.

One trial learning's usually take place when we simultaneously experience an intense or high emotional level. This ability of the human brain to learn quickly provides opportunity for us to experience truly rapid change.

19. All communication should increase choice:

This NLP presupposition believes that the more choice an individual has, the more wholeness that individual experiences. Indeed, a great way to break rapport with an individual results when you remove choice.

Give them choice and they experience happiness. Speaking therapeutically, most problems we confront in working with people consist of their being trapped in some perceived problem.

They live at what we call the "effect" of some perceived "cause." The more choice you give a person or yourself the more satisfaction they experience.

20. People make the best choices open to them when they act:

How frequently do we experience high levels of frustration with people because we do not understand the choices they make? How many times do we scratch our heads and say, "Don't they know better? What's wrong with them?"

Thinking-feeling and saying such indicates our frame of reference: "Others should operate from my model of the world" frame! This presupposition shifts that. Here we start from the working assumption that people come from their own model of the world and that they make the best choices available to them in that model.

Starting from the assumption that people make the best choices available to them at the time enables us to approach them with compassion, to forgive them. This fosters gentleness, kindness, optimism, and hope. People make stupid, ugly and destructive choices while thinking that somehow it will make things better for them.

Realizing this about others and ourselves enables us to treat everyone with more kindness and gentleness about our human fallibility and stupidity. This realization supports the value and importance of forgiveness. Imagine for a moment what would follow if you held this belief toward the members of your family?

What would result if you practiced this presupposition with the people at work? With your friends? With clients? Doing so will obviously affect the way you communicate with your significant others.

It's about being non judgmental about people doing the best they think they can.

21. We can run our brains & control our results:

Your brain is like a machine without an "off" switch. If you don't give it something to do, it just runs on and on until it gets bored. (Think about late at night when you can't sleep because you have something on your mind.)

If you put someone in a sensory deprivation tank where there's no external experience, he'll start generating internal experience. If your brain is sitting around without anything to do, it's going to start doing something, and it doesn't seem to care what it is. You may care, but it doesn't.

If you don't give your brain a little direction, either it will just run randomly on its own, or other people will find ways to run it for you—and they may not always have your best interests in mind.

Now you know the operational system of beliefs and values that drives the NLP model—a reality frame of presuppositions about how the human mind-body system works. In NLP, we simply start from these assumptions rather than spend lots of time studying, "proving," deleting, validating, etc., them.

Frames

In NLP the process of framing refers to the putting
of things in different contexts (frames of reference)
in order to give them different meanings.

First we will study some of the primary frames of
reference as presented in NLP.

The "As If" frame

Provides a valuable communication tool when
dealing with people who resist change. Pretending
as a rule does not create as threatening an
environment as when we face real change. Since
the frame tends to remove the threatening aspects
of change, people's minds become open to new
choices.

1. Time Switch: Pretend that you have moved six
months or a year into a successful future. Then,
look back and ask yourself, "What steps did I take
that led me to this successful outcome?"

2. Person Switch: "If you could become anyone you wanted to become, who or what would you become and how would they handle this problem?"

3. Information Switch: "Let's just suppose that you had all the information you needed, then what do you suppose...?"

4. Function Switch: "Just pretend that you could change any part of the situation...

Context Reframe

Separate the intention from the behaviour.
Since every behaviour is appropriate in some context, think of a different context in which the person's behaviour would be appropriate.

"It is appropriate to use physical force to restrain a suspect or in self-defence, but it is not appropriate to use physical force just because you are angry at the suspect."

Meaning Reframe

"Whenever X, I respond to Y". Separate the intention from the behaviour.
What else could the behaviour mean? What hasn't this person noticed that will bring about different meaning?

"Whenever he uses that tone with me, I get angry and defensive."

"Is it possible that when he uses that tone, it just means that he's in a hurry to get something done?"

The Relevancy Frame

Asking the person how something is relevant will uncover information that you can use to persuade them.

Outcome: person wants to lose weight.

"I watch too much TV."
"How is this relevant? How does this relate to what you want to achieve?"

Contrast Frame

Using the contrast frame, you are challenging a person to look beyond their map.

Remember to keep rapport, this is a challenging reframe.
"I want this to be better."
"Better compared to what?"
"I need more energy."

"More than what?"

The Agreement Frame

Use this model as a way to gain agreement with another person. Avoid using the word "understand" and the word "but".

"I appreciate your point of view, and..."
"I respect what you are saying, and...'
"I agree with a part of your point, and..."

The Purpose Frame

If you find out someone's purpose, you can persuade them by adjusting your communication to highlight the ways in which what you are proposing fits their purpose.

It also helps the listener clarify their purpose.

"I want to be able to do this." "For what purpose?"

The Would / Won't Happen Frame

Using this frame, you will direct the person's mind to open up possibilities they may have not thought about before.

"I can't change"
"What would happen if you did?"
"What would happen when you make that change?"

"What would happen if you didn't make that change?"
"What won't happen when you make that change?"
"What won't happen if you didn't make that change?"

Reframing

If you change the context, meaning or content, you can change the meaning!

The two major kinds of reframes that we learn at the Practitioner level are the Context Reframe and the Meaning Reframe.

A classic example of a reframe by Virginia Satir concerns a father who complains at the stubbornness of his daughter.

This results in a double reframe, in which Satir points out two things to the father:

1. There are situations where she will need stubbornness to protect herself, or achieve something. Reframing switches to a context that makes the stubbornness relevant.

93

2. It is from the father himself that she has learned to be stubborn. By forcing the father to equate his own stubbornness with hers, this creates a context in which he either has to recognize the value of her stubbornness, or deny the value of his own.

Reframing is a powerful change stratagem.

It changes our perceptions, and this may then affect our actions.

Well Formed Outcomes - Goal Setting

In recent decades, many have written about the process of effectively setting goals.

You may be familiar with the S.M.A.R.T. goals:

S- Specific
M - Measurable
A - Attainable/Assignable
R - Realistic/Rewarding
T - Timetable/Tangible

Goal setting functions as a prerequisite to success in most areas of life. Yet amazingly many people still do not set goals.

The POWER MIND NLP model allows us to go beyond mere "goal setting" into desired outcome development.

A goal after all is something you aim for whereby an outcome is something that happens. Here we do not talk just about setting goals but about setting outcomes. How do they differ? Goals are described in general terms, outcomes in specifics.

Once you have taken a goal through the well-formed outcome model, you greatly increase the probability of achieving your outcome.

The specificity of the well-formed outcome model facilitates concentration on what you internally see, hear, and feel. Your attention will direct itself toward external and internal resources necessary in achieving the outcome. POWER MIND IS ABOUT RADICALLY FAST INSTANT CHANGES FOR PERMANENT FIX CHANGES

POWER MIND

Few of us hold more than two or three items in our mind, consciously, at a time. Our minds must select.

A well-formed outcome enables us to create specific pictures, sounds, feelings and words. Then that image activates our abilities and resources for achieving that outcome.

This empowers us to take advantage of what we find presently available in our environment to attain our outcome.

The well-formed outcome model aids us in specifying who we will become. The model will enable us in the development of an image that we find both achievable and appropriate.

Often people ask, "Isn't this just positive thinking?"

We explain, "Not exactly, for while positive thinking obviously helps, NLP goes beyond mere positive thinking to providing a way to think productively.

A well-formed outcome should have the following characteristics

1. Stated positively in terms of what we want (NOT what we don't and what we don't want others to give us)

2. Described in sensory-based language.

3. Self-initiated and self-controlled.

4. Appropriate (Congruent)

5. Maintains appropriate secondary gain.

6. Builds in/includes the needed resources.

7. Ecological for the whole system.

1. State Positively

The human mind does not directly process a negative.

If I ask you not to think of a green kangaroo to process that statement, you will have to think by mentally representing the aforementioned green kangaroo.

You may then try to negate it by crossing it out, letting it fade away, etc., but first you have to represent it. If you tell a child to not spill their drink, then first of all, the child will probably see themselves "spilling their rink." And children, unfortunately, often forget to negate the representation after creating it.

The way we use our mental processing informs us about how and why we often end up doing exactly the opposite of what we ask of others or ourselves.

We need to ask ourselves, "What kind of image does my question or statement create in the mind?" So our outcome describes what we positively want to accomplish. It describes something you want, not what you don't want. We feel far more motivated to accomplish a positive outcome than a negative outcome. So we should not state outcomes using negations: "I am going to stop smoking."

That describes what we aim to not do (a negation). Every time you think of your outcome of stopping smoking, you internally imagine doing that very thing you want to stop doing. You have to think of what you don't want to be doing—smoking. And, as we think, so we will become.

We should phrase it as a positive outcome: "I will take care of my health."

To think of this outcome, we imagine looking and feeling healthy. And if we think (represent) health, we will more likely experience health since we continue to send positive messages not only to our "mind," but also to our neurology.

We also recommend that in your visualization of your outcome you make the image of yourself having your outcome dissociated. So, once you have created an image of yourself having your outcome, make sure you see yourself in the picture.

Why? Well, think of it this way: if you formulate your outcome associated (you do not see yourself in the picture), then your brain will tell your body that you already have your outcome.
The reason— the brain does not know the difference between imagination and reality.

Exercise: Do this test. See for yourself the power of your imagination.

Imagine a fruit bowl stacked with fruit, really large and filled with delicious, colourful fruits.

Imagine the oranges, the deep green and reds of the apples, the warm sunshine yellow bananas, the peaches and pears.

You can almost smell their heady aroma.

Now from the fruit bowl you reach forward and pick up a large, ripe, lemon.

Now imagine yourself going over to your counter and taking out a knife and cutting board.

Next, slice the lemon in half, then in quarters. Afterwards, pick up a one-quarter slice of lemon as you pick the lemon up you realize how ripe and juicy it is.

It is almost like you can smell its freshness and feel the oozing juice running sickly over your fingers.

Now slowly bring the lemon towards yourself, open your mouth and NOW take a great big bite!
Was your mouth watering? For most people, this simple exercise will cause your mouth to water.

How come? After all, you don't have a lemon in your mouth. It happens because through the processes of imagination your brain activated your salivary glands and your mouth watered.

Your mind remembers the taste of lemons and it has simply recalled the associated sensations linked to the action of eating a lemon and caused your body to respond in what it deems an appropriate way.

Likewise, if you recall your outcome images associated, your brain will instruct your body that you already have the outcome—and you will not have as much motivation to obtain your outcome as you will if you recall it dissociated. Your brain will tell your body from a dissociated position, "I want that. I don't now have it but I can have it. Let's go get it!"

It does not even matter that you may not know how to reach the outcome your unconscious mind will work for you and direct you in an appropriate way.

You do after all have your own best interests at heart. When you run your brain with intent you will truly move towards what is best for you.

To begin designing some well-formed outcomes, use the following questions to formulate your outcome (or a client's outcome).

These questions assist in establishing a
well-formed outcome:

- What specifically do you want?
- What will having that do for you?
- Have you stated your outcome positively?
- Do you see yourself having your outcome?

2. Described in sensory-based language

Using sensory language and that means engaging
not just preferred and lead sensory systems but as
many as possible.

Now ask, "What will I see, hear and feel when I have
my outcome?"

This step will let us know when we have our
outcome—our evidence procedure. In NLP, we base
outcomes on sensory experience (seeing, hearing,
and feeling).

Why? Because the mind processes information in
these terms.

Our individual skills arise from how we develop
and sequence our representational systems. In
other words, we will reach our outcome through
the mental processes of creating an internal map of
our outcome in terms of sights, sounds, and
sensations—what we will see, hear, and feel.

These processes, in turn, determine our internal state.

And our internal state coupled with our physiology ultimately drives our behaviour. And by means of our behaviour, we create our outcome.

Further, code the desired outcome in a dissociated image so that you see, hear, and feel it as "out there."

This will set up a neurological direction so that you will have a feeling of wanting to move toward it.

- How will you know when you achieve your outcome?
- What will you see when you have your outcome?
- What will you hear when you have your outcome?
- What will you feel when you have your outcome?

3. Self-initiated and self-controlled

While we can control our own thinking-and-emoting responses to life, we cannot control other people—especially their thoughts-and-emotions.

Often we hear someone ask, "How can I change my spouse's behaviour?"

Easy

"Change your behaviour and responses in some way that leaves your spouse without the need for their old program. Now what do you need to do that?"

Changing others directly lies outside our control. Changing them indirectly by changing ourselves—we can do that!

The well-formed outcome works with changes that we can initiate, maintain, and manage. To put our outcome at the disposal of others only disempowers us and invites failure.

- Do you and you alone control your outcome?
- Does your outcome involve anyone else?
- Can you both initiate & maintain the responses needed to reach your outcome?

4. Appropriate (Congruent)

We need to design our well-formed outcome to fit into all the appropriate contexts of our lives.

When we fail to do such, we build an over-generalized outcome that can cause problems in other areas. So we ask,

- Where and when do you want this particular outcome?

- Under what conditions?
- What other constraints of time, energy, context, etc., do you need to consider as you build the outcome representations?"
- In what situations would having your outcome become inappropriate
- Or useless?
- Where, when, how & with whom do you want this outcome?
- Do you want my outcome all the time, in all places and without any limitations?

5. Maintains appropriate secondary gain.

All of our present behaviour provides us with positive values and outcomes. If it didn't, we would not perpetuate and maintain it.

In psychology, clinicians refer to this feedback as "secondary gain." We talk about this in NLP as the ecology of the entire system (a personal, human system of thoughts, emotions, relationships, etc.).

A person who smokes gains something from smoking. If they did not, they would not smoke. An individual who eats too much gains something from overeating. If they did not, they would not over- eat.

Therefore in changing behaviour, if we do not preserve these secondary gains, and provide alternative ways of attaining them, the desired behaviour changes will probably not last. This undoubtedly explains why so much change doesn't last.

Use the following questions to discover the secondary gains you may have hidden inside your current behaviours:

- What would you lose if you accomplished your outcome?
- When, where & with whom would not having your outcome feel OK?
- Would you have to give up anything that you deem important to have this outcome?

6. Builds in/includes the needed resources.

To reach our desired outcomes—we need resources.

A well-formed outcome will therefore have the needed resources included within it so that we imagine and represent such as part of the outcome achievement.

Many people set goals which they simultaneously "can't imagine" themselves really experiencing!

This indicates that they have not built in the needed resources.

- What do you have now, and what do you need, to get your outcome?

- Have you ever done this before?
- Do you know anyone who has done this before?

7. Ecological for the whole system.

Ecology, as the science of the relationship between an organism and its environment, in NLP speaks about our concern that changes made at one point in a human system must fit together with, and adapt to, the other parts of the system in a healthy way.

In defining a well-formed outcome, we therefore give consideration both to the individual and to other people in the system.

Human systems include family, work relationships, school, friends and community. If we gain from one area at the expense of another area, this benefit will not last. NLP says that "We need to evaluate behaviour and change in terms of context and ecology."

The following four questions derive from Cartesian logic.

These four questions offer some useful and powerful linguistic patterns. The theory of

Cartesian logic asserts that if an outcome (or any theory) will hold true in all four questions, then you can view your outcome as attainable.

As you process your outcome through these questions, notice if you get a negative internal feeling (K1") or an objecting thought.

I have done Power Mind for tens of thousands of people.
Removing thoughts energetic patterns that caused the stubborn objecting thoughts.

All minds can be programmed to benefit the true Goal of why you were born.

So I will repeat the scientific As you process your outcome through these questions, notice if you get a negative internal feeling (K1") or an objecting thought.

If so, you probably will need to alter your outcome until you have positive thought-feelings about outcome. These questions provide a powerful means of discovering if your outcome truly fits your needs. You may want to memorize these questions and see just how helpful they become in your communications and change work:

- What will happen if you get it?
- What won't happen if you get it?
- What will happen if you don't get it?

- What won't happen if you don't get it?

Other sample questions that may assist in forming your own well formed outcomes are:

- Can I test the outcome?
- Can I feel the outcome?
- Can I chunk down the outcome into achievable pieces'!
- We should give special care to avoid making our outcomes too global.

In a well-formed outcome, we need to break the outcome down into a step-by-step procedure.

Such will then allow us to achieve the outcome via a systematic, patterned and teachable way.

- Do / know the first step to take?
- Do I feel I can achieve the first step?
- If I reached the outcome would it fit with my values?
- Can I find more than one way to achieve the outcome?
- What appropriate personal anchors exist in the context in which I desire the outcome?
- Do I have sufficient information about the internal state necessary for reaching the outcome?
- Do I have the image of the outcome firmly in my mind?

- Do I have the sounds, pictures, words and feelings of the desired outcome in mind?
- Does my internal state drive my behaviour in the direction of obtaining the outcome?

Well Formedness Conditions for Outcomes/Goals

1. Stated in positive terms.
2. Initiated and maintained by the client.
3. Specific sensory-based description of outcome and the steps needed to get there.
4. Ecological.
5. More than one way to get the outcome.
6. First step is specified and achievable.
7. Does it increase choice?

Meta Model

The Meta-model in Neuro-linguistic programming (NLP) is a model of (primarily) linguistic models that people have.

"Meta" comes from Greek and means "beyond, over, about, on a different level."

Put simply in this context, the meta-model is a set of language patterns (from Virginia Satir, Fritz Perls and Transformational syntax) designed to challenge limits to a person's internal map of the world.

The Meta-model specifies how we can use language to clarify language.

Effectively the meta-model can be reduced to asking "What specifically", or "How specifically?" to challenge unspecified nouns or verbs.

The Meta-model provides us with a tool to get to the experience behind a person's words.

When we speak, none of us gives a complete description of the thoughts behind our words. We have to use verbal shortcuts or we would never finish speaking.

We will always have a more complete internal representation of what we wish to communicate than what we can put into words. We inevitably shorten the description.

The reverse of the meta-model is the Milton-model; a collection of artfully vague language patterns elicited from the work of Milton Erickson.

Together these models form the basis for the all other NLP models.

The internal representation in all its glorious non verbal detail we refer to as "Deep Structure".

Much of this will lay within our unconscious minds and embedded in our neurology. Explaining the concept of "Love" for example has been a challenge to the greatest writers and poets for centuries, yet we instinctively know when we feel this emotion.

As we seek to present, articulate and clarify our experiences, we do so in what we call "Surface Structures" - the words and sentences that represent transforms of the deeper levels.

Bandler and Grinder noted that in the process of moving from the Deep Structure in our neurology (our neurological "map") to the Surface Structures that come out of our conscious minds and mouths, we do three things, which they termed "modelling processes."

For the most part, we do this naturally and apart from consciousness.

First, we delete much if not most of the material in the Deep Structure. Every second, approximately two million pieces of information feed into the brain.

Second, we distort the meaning and structure of information as we simplify our description of the experience. We alter our perceptions using our brains.

A story in Eastern philosophy relates how a man walked along the road and saw a snake. Immediately he yelled, "Snake!" But then, as he approached it, he saw it more clearly as a rope, and not a snake.

Third, we generalize information. When new learning's come into our brain, our brain compares the new information with similar information previously learned.

Our minds compare and generalize old similar material with new data. This process allows us to learn quickly.

In summary, we delete, distort and generalize information as we create our model of the world.

The Meta Model is the basis for being able to model excellence. It is a means for uncovering the structure of a person's thinking processes and perceptions. All of us have very unique ways in which we organize and describe the world around us, and few of us understand how it works to shape our world.

By using the Meta Model, you will be able uncover the deletions, distortions and generalizations in another person's thinking process.

You will discover what they absolutely will not accept and what they would consider a possibility.

Learn to make critical distinctions in language.

This is very important because the more precise distinctions you make the more influential you will be.

Great artists, painters, sculptors, architects and designers are able to observe and make more discriminations visually than the average person.

Talented composers make more distinctions about sounds, melody, and rhythm. Athletes make more distinctions about their body, feelings, movements and timing.

Just like these great talents, you will become sensitized to making more distinctions in the area of language.

Since all of us use language it makes sense that those most successful have learned to make distinctions in language that others have not.

These successful people know when and how to ask the right questions to get them the information that they need. They negotiate better, they are more in tune with the needs of their clients and families, and they understand the meaning of the words that other's speak.

Distortion is the seat of your creativity. It is the place where you can create or "distort" what you see, hear and feel and make it even better or make it worse.

Distortion is what makes it possible to imagine and create things. Distortions are also what allow two people to have completely different interpretations of the same event.

Think for example about the differing eye witness accounts at a road traffic accident.

Taking this to an extreme where would the focus be of a nurse at such an accident compared to say a car mechanic?

Deletion cuts out the information you don't need according to your filters. It decides what is most important for you to keep and what needs to be left out.

Deletion allows us to be able to go through the world without sensory overload. Every second we are being bombarded with information through our senses, over 2 million pieces of information every single second.

We only process approximately 7 pieces of this information (+/- 2). An example would be that it is unlikely that you would be aware of the rate that you are swallowing until it is brought to your conscious awareness by reading this sentence.

Of course this was an automated response in your body and was occurring without any conscious intervention or awareness. You just did not need to be aware of it.

Generalization is the organizer.

This is where you compare the experience to what you've experienced before and pull everything together in one big theme or idea.

Generalization allows us to make sense of experience and understand things. It also allows us to make sweeping assumptions that may not be based on fact.

Just based on similar previous experience.

The secret of the Meta Model is:

1. Listen to what they say.
2. Construct a representation of that in your own mind – one which is based only on what they say.

3. Ask yourself: What's missing? What or who is being limited? What just doesn't make sense?

The Secret of General Modelling is:

1. Listen to and look closely at everything they present you with.

2. Form a tentative model, or hypothesis about what they do - one which is based on what they offer you.

3. Ask yourself: What is missing? What else has to be there? Is this enough to succeed at what the person can do so well? Or do I need to find out more?

Nominalizations

Linguistically, nominalization refers to changing a Deep Structure process (movement, action, etc.) into a Surface Structure static event.

The classic NLP description that tests for a nominalization versus a true noun asks:
"Can you put it in a wheelbarrow?"

If so, you have a noun!

If not, then behold a nominalization!

Nominalizations delete large amounts of information.

Consider the statement, "Our poor relationship really bothers me."

"Relationship" functions as a nominalization, even though we generally treat it as a concrete noun.

But we cannot see, hear, smell, or taste a relationship.

We can't put a relationship in a wheelbarrow.

Changing the verb "relating" into the pseudo- noun "relationship," nominalizes the verb.

Other examples of nominalizations: education, illness, respect, discipline, friendship, decision, love, fear, strategy and sensation.

To challenge nominalizations, we reverse the process.

As a person has changed a process into a thing, we now direct him or her to change the thing back into a process.

We do that by using the format: "In what way do you do the process of (nominalization)?"

This question then assists the person to reconnect with the experience in a way that recognizes their role in the process.

Examples are:
I have a poor relationship.
You have no respect for me.
Our system of education stinks.
Communication is a problem in their marriage
Management made poor decisions.
His desires got him into trouble.
Her behaviour is unacceptable.
This exercise will provide you with new insights,
and new understandings.

Mind Reading

We engage in mind reading when we think and
assert that we know the thoughts, motives,
intentions, etc., in another's mind.

We do this when we say, "I know exactly how you
feel."

In spite of communicating sympathy, typically such
statements trigger pain, resentment,
misunderstanding, etc.

Mind-reading Surface Structure reveals much
more about the speaker's internal experience than
the others.

Accordingly, when we utter mind reading
statements, we project our own perceptions,
values, issues, history, etc. Thus they usually have
little to do with the person to whom we speak.

To challenge mind reading, ask, "How specifically do you know how I feel (think, intend, etc.)?" In response to the is question, the speaker will then offer more of their internal world-model (Deep Structure).

The question will allow the speaker to question assumptions and recover the source of the information.

Examples are:
I know he doesn't care.
She knows better.
I'm sure you're aware...
I can tell you don't like me.
He isn't interested.
You think...
You're upset.
I know that you are wondering

Cause-Effect

The over-used accusation, "You make me mad!" illustrates a cause-effect statement.

This sentence implies that you directly make or cause me to feel mad as if I have no choice in the process.

However you create this effect when you do, I must feel this way.

It seems to imply that you have a kind of psychic power over me.

Words that indicate the presence of cause-effect statements include: make, if then, as you..., then, because, and almost any present tense verb.

To challenge such statements, ask, "How specifically do I cause you to feel bad?" "By what process do I 'make' you have these feelings, thoughts, or responses?" "Do you have no choice whatever in how you respond to this stimulus?"

Such responses invite the speaker to expand and enhance their map about cause-and-effect in human relationships.

It empowers the speaker to take responsibility for their own feelings, thoughts, and responses.

It facilitates the speaker to adopt a more proactive response by exploring their choices.

One of the larger-level purposes of therapy involves empowering a client to recognize their response-able powers and to own their responses as their own.

Clients generally feel that they suffer the effects of the causes of others.

Effective counselling leads them to realize how
they also stand 'at cause/ so we lead them to take
control of their own lives and responses as they
claim their own powers: the power to think, feel,
speak, and behave.
Examples are:

I'm late because of you.
When you believe in me, I can do it.
You make me feel.
I would do it, but I'm mad.
I feel badly that I hurt him.
Just asking that question you begin to understand.
When we challenge our Cause-Effect(s) (and
others) we dissociate ourselves (and others) from
our boxes and give ourselves permission to ask,
"Does this type of thinking serve me (you)?"

Complex Equivalence

We generate a complex equivalence whenever we
use a part of an experience (an aspect of the
external behaviour) to become equivalent to the
whole of its meaning (our internal state).

Thus when we become aware of the external cue,
we then assume the meaning of the whole
experience. "You did not tell me that you love me
this morning; you just don't love me anymore."

Here a person has equated certain external behaviours (saying words that express love to someone) and an internal state (feeling loved).

The construction of complex equivalences utilize words of equation.

A person makes one external phenomenon identical with another internal phenomenon.

We challenge a complex equivalence by asking about the equation, "How specifically does my not telling you that I love you (EB) mean that I don't love you anymore (IS)?" "Have I ever failed to tell you that I loved you and yet you knew that I truly did love you?"

Such questioning enables the speaker to identify the complex equivalent belief and recover additional material deleted and distorted.

We can take any statement a person gives us in whatever form and them,

"What does that mean to you?" and we will chunk down on their statement towards the first level meaning they have given to their Internal Representations.

If you believe they haven't chunked down specific enough, just repeat, "And, what does that mean to

you?" This will direct the person to describe more
in detail the meaning of their statement.

Examples are:
Joe's face is red. That must mean he is angry.
Being here means you will change.
Going to bed early means you will be alert.
You know the answer, so you are competent.
Sitting in this room, you are learning many things.
As you master these skills, you will be a better
communicator.
Keeping your eyes open like that means you'll go
into trance.
And closing your eyes means you'll go even deeper.

Presuppositions

By the term presupposition, we refer to the
conceptual and linguistic assumptions that have to
exist in order for a statement to make sense.

By definition, we do not state our presuppositions
- they operate rather as the supporting foundation
or context of a given statement.

In presuppositions we find the person's beliefs
about life, the world, self, others, God, etc. And we
all operate from specific presuppositions. So when
we learn to listen for presuppositions we can hear
a lot about the person's model of the world.

Presuppositions function similarly to Mind-Reads.

They just leave out the "I know." Any
non-sensory-specific language will contain
presuppositions.

Presuppositions in language work covertly,
indirectly, and unconsciously as we have to accept
them and their assumptions in order to make
sense of the communication.
A presupposition can operate positively as with the
fundamental Christian belief that God loves every
person.
And some presuppositions can impose limitations
on us. Many presuppositions that limit us begin
with "why" questions. We can also learn to listen for
such terms as: since, when, if, etc.

The sentence: "Why don't you work harder?"
presupposes that the recipient does not work hard
enough. "If you only knew you would understand
my pain" presupposes the recipient does not
understand the speaker's pain.

To challenge a presupposition, inquire about the
assumptions in the statement.
"What leads you to believe that I don't work hard
enough? Hard enough according to what standard?
"What leads you to believe that I don't know your
pain?" "How specifically do you assume I need to
work harder?" Or, "How would you like me to
specifically understand your pain?" What

125

presuppositions lie in this? "You have learned a lot about presuppositions."

"How excited do you now feel having learned about the Meta-model and its powerful questions?"
"When do you think you would best like to study and practice learning the Meta-model to become even more proficient?"

Examples are:
We have talked about presuppositions.
You are learning about the Meta-model and the powerful questions the
Meta-model gives us.
If you would study and practice, you would learn the Meta-model.
You can d o this even better.
You are changing all the time.
How else do you go into connection verses trance?
You're seeing things differently now.
You'll be able to learn even more tomorrow.
You realize you have more resources than ever before.
You can easily move in the direction of your past memories.
Most of the examples of this pattern will be written here by you
You are learning many things.

Universal Quantifiers

A universal quantifier refers to the set of words that make a universal generalization.

They imply a state of absoluteness—of "allness." In this generalization we make one category represent a whole group.

Thus we move from "Dad abused me at seven years of age/" to "Men always abuse."

This statement generalizes from a particular to the whole class.

Generalizations have no reference point. They are intentionally vague.

Universal quantifiers consist of such words as: all, never, every, always and none.

Such words do not leave room for any exceptions.

By definition they express a limited mindset. The Meta-model challenge to a universal quantifier involves simply repeating the word back to the person in the form of a question.
To "All men are abusers" we could respond: "All?" Another challenge involves asking if the speaker has ever met a man who did not abuse. This challenge brings out the absurdity of the universal quantifier.

Examples are:

All Christians are hypocrites.
Every politician is a liar.
Everyone on welfare is lazy.
Nobody's perfect.
Everything is wonderful.
We are all in trance now.
There is always tomorrow.
Everybody knows this part is easy.
One can never know all there is to know.
All of the people doing this process are learning
many new things
And all the things, all the things...

Modal Operators

This linguistic distinction refers to our mode whereby we operate in the world.
Do we operate from a mental world of laws (should, must, have to); do we operate from a world of opportunities (possible, possible to, can); do we operate from a world of obligations (ought, should); or empowerment (dare, want to, desire to), etc.?

In other words these modal operator terms define the boundaries of our model of the world and our style of operation.

So words like can and cannot, should and should not reveal personal beliefs about what we can or cannot do in life.

Now modal operators come in several categories. We have the modal operators of necessity, of possibility, impossibility, empowerment, identity, choice, etc. These modes show up in words like can/cannot, possible/impossible, am/am not, and will/will not, etc.

Listening for such words informs us what a client believes stands as possible or impossible in their world. "I can't change my beliefs." "I can't learn efficiently." "I can't imagine saying that." Such language not only describes their limits, it creates such limitations.

Modal operators of possibility tell us what a person believes possible.

The Meta-model challenge to such goes: "What would happen if you did change that belief?" Or, "What stops you from doing that?" Fritz Perls reframed "I can't..." by saying, 'Don't say I can't, say I won't."

If a client accepted that statement, they moved from no choice to choice, from effect of a problem to the cause of such. All of therapy has to do with putting the client at cause. The presupposition in the phrase, "Don't say I can't, say I won't," assumes that the client can choose.

Necessity words include: must/must not, should/should not, ought/ought not, have to, need to and it is necessary.

These describe a model of the world that believes in necessity. Such words define some governing rule the person operates from. Often these rules limit behaviour.

Telling children that they should do their homework can induce a state of guilt (pseudo-guilt). Modal operators of necessity work wonderfully for creating such guilt.

Yet if guiltiness doesn't strike you as a particularly resourceful place to come from for studying, instead of telling children that they should do their homework, we can tell them that they can do their homework. "And I get to help you with it."

The Meta-model challenge to a modal operator of necessity: "What would happen if you did/didn't...?" "I should go to church!" Response: "What would happen if you did go?" This will elicit specific reasons why they should go to church.

The question goes to the Deep Structure and facilitates the person to recover effects and outcome. It moves the client into the future. Examples: "I really should be more flexible at times like this." "I ought to go back to school." "I have to take care of her." "You should learn."

These questions come from Cartesian Logic. One can introduce this unique form of questioning by saying, "You have been thinking about this one way for quite a while and your thinking hasn't changed. May I suggest another line of thinking? (Get their agreement either verbally or non-verbally) What would happen if you did change that belief?" etc.

Examples: Modal Operators of Necessity:
I really should be more flexible at times like this.
I ought to go back to school.
You should not hurry into trance just yet.
You shouldn't go into trance too quickly, now.
You must be getting this now... at some level...
I have to take care of her.

You should learn.
Examples: Modal Operators of
Possibility/Impossibility:
I can't learn.
I couldn't tell him what I think.
You could learn this now.
You could write this down... or not.
You could feel more and more peaceful.
You can change overnight.
You may hear the words of wisdom.
It's possible to learn everything easily and quickly.

Lost Performative

When we perform upon our world with value
judgments, we speak about important values that
we believe in.

But in a Lost Performative we have stated a value
judgment while deleting the performer (speaker) of
the value judgment. As a vague value judgment, a
Lost Performative will push the person into the
direction you wish for them to go. "You don't love
me."

Note that the value judgment leaves off the name of
the person doing the judging but it directs
attention to "love me."

"Boys shouldn't cry" "If you're going to do
something, give it your best."

"That is a stupid thing you just did."

In these sentences the speaker has made a value judgment about something. Yet statements fail to inform us who said such or where the person got that value judgment.

To challenge a lost performative and restore the deleted and distorted material, ask: "Who says boys shouldn't cry?" "Who evaluates my actions as stupid?" "According to whom do you say such?" Or even more succinctly, ask, "Says who?"

These questions require that the speaker access more information in the Deep Structure and identify the source of the judgments.

Until we identify the source, we will lack the ability to challenge the statement's validity.

Examples are:
Oh, it's not important anyway
It's not good to be strict.
That's too bad.
Today is a great day,
No one should judge others.
That's perfect!
It's really good that you say that.
One doesn't have to...
And, it is a good thing to wonder.

Simple Deletions

A simple deletion occurs when the communicator leaves out information
About a person, thing or relationship.
Examples are:
I am uncomfortable
I feel afraid.
I am hurting.
I feel alone.
I don't know.

Comparative Deletions

In a comparative deletion someone makes a comparison, but deletes either the specific persons, things, or items compared or the standard by which the speaker makes the comparison.

Words like better, best, further, nearer, richer, poorer, more, less, most, least, worse, etc., provide cues of comparative deletions.

What you compare to functions as a presupposition and the other person's unconscious mind will fill in what's missing.

"He is much better off." The challenge: "Better off than who?" "Better off according to what standard?"

Examples are:
He is the best student in the class.
And it is more or less the right thing to do.

Lack of Referential Index or Unspecified Nouns and Verbs

By referential index we refer to the person or thing that does or receives the action from the verb in the statement. When a sentence lacks a referential index, it fails to specify by name, term, or phrase that it references—whom it speaks about. It fails to specify or point to a specific person or group. The pronouns (one, it, they, people, etc.) are unspecified. Crucial material from the Deep Structure that completes the meaning has been deleted.

Listen for words like one, they, nobody and this. "They did not come to the meeting." Here the speaker failed to specify the subject of the verb. To challenge and recover the deleted material, we ask, "Who specifically did not come to the meeting?" In the statement, "Those people hurt me" the noun phrase ("those people") like the unspecified verb ("hurt") lacks a referential index. So we inquire, "Who specifically hurt you?"

Examples are:

They don't listen to me
Nobody cares anymore
This is unheard of.
One can, you know.

Unspecified Verb

Unspecified verbs describe vague, non-specific action.

Words like hurt, upset, injure, show, demonstrate, care and concern certainly describe action, a process, a set of events or experiences—but they have left out so much of the specific information about the action that we cannot make a clear representation in our mind about that action.

She says, "He hurt me," but we don't know if he slapped her, left her waiting at the mall, molested her, insulted the pie she baked, etc.

We recover such deleted material by asking, "How did he hurt you exactly?

"Who specifically hurt you?" If we fail to ask for the deleted information, we run the risk of inventing it in our own minds!
While we may make good guesses if we know enough of the context and background, we may also make guesses that miss the other person's meaning by light years.

When we hear a sentence with an unspecified verb ("She misunderstood me"), the potential exists for much misunderstanding, because we can interpret it in many different ways.

The questions will connect the person more fully to their experience. In terms of well-formedness we do not provide a sufficient enough linguistic "map" for the other person to get a clear message.

Examples are:
You don't care about me.
I upset my mother.
He doesn't show me any concern
I was wondering.
If only you knew.
You may discover.
And you can learn this.
Deletions

Most sentences in our everyday language contain numerous Meta-model violations. As you hear them, start at the larger level violation and challenge the distortions first.

Then go to the generalizations. And finally, challenge the deletions.

Every sentence has lots of deletions, if you start there, you could challenge deletions all day long.

Since distortions carry the most weight and operate at a higher logical level, when we challenge them first, we get greater leverage on the person's Deep Structure.

You can now begin to use this Meta-model to enable you to get specific information in a client's, colleagues, family, anyone in fact - their Deep Structure.

The questions provided by the Meta-model enable you to chunk the person down to details and specificity.

As such, the Meta-model facilitates the uncovering of crucial information which then empowers one to expand their world-model.

At the same time, the questions of the Meta-model function to essentially bring a client out of trance. To put a client in trance, we would use the reverse language patterns, and in NLP, the reverse patterns show up in a model that we call the Milton Model.

Milton Model

After developing the Meta-model Bandler and
Grinder met Milton Erickson, the world-renowned
medical hypnotherapist and founder of the
American Society for Clinical Hypnosis.

Grinder reported that Erickson provided him with
the single greatest model he has ever used.

Erickson opened an entire new area of thought in
therapy and communication.

From their study of Erickson, they soon after
published Patterns of Hypnotic Techniques of
Milton H. Erickson Volume I.

Later, Volume 2 (1977) Bandler and Grinder learned from Erickson the value of trance and altered states in therapy.

Many of the NLP presuppositions come from Erickson's work.

He respected the client's unconscious mind, and believed that positive intention drives all behaviours, that individuals make best choices available to them, that people have the resources within to make their desired changes, etc.

Much of the rapport building techniques of NLP come from Erickson's genius at building and maintaining rapport (pacing and leading).

As the Meta-model steps down to specifics to recover distorted, generalized, and deleted materials, this takes us out of trance.

The Milton Model conversely chunks up to make new generalizations, deletions, and distortions.

Rather than go for specific information, it steps up to general information— to the big picture.

The Milton model mirrors in reverse the Metamodel.
Expect to find lots of distortions, generalizations, and deletions in this model.

140

Here we intentionally use language to give the
client room to fill in the pieces.

We provide an open frame with little context so
that the client's unconscious mind will activate an
internal search.

General language inherently induces one to go into
a trance on this search.

So the language patterns within the Milton model
facilitates this process.

Because the Milton model mirrors in reverse the
Meta-model, we put a person in trance by using
the Meta-model violations.

Here we do not ask questions for questions invite
the mind to come up (into uptime).

We aim to creatively use Meta-model violations to
induce a trance state: "I know (mind read) that you
have begun to gain new learning's (nominalization)
about a great many subjects (unspecified noun) of
significance to you. And, it is a good thing to learn
(lost performative), to really learn... For, as you gain
new learning's (presupposition), you have already
begun to change (cause-effect) and I don't know
how you feel that, now... but you can. And, the fact
that you have begun to change in ever so slight
ways means that healing (complex equivalence) has

141

begun. And you might experience these changes (presuppositions) by how you feel or just by how you talk to yourself. Since you have begun to make changes (nominalization) that means all (universal quantifier) other areas needing healing can begin to change (entire sentence a complex equivalence.).

And you can change (modal operator of possibility and unspecified verb), as you should (modal operator of necessity). It is more or less the right thing to do
(lost performative), that is to change (comparative deletion)."

In addition to these Meta-model categories, the Milton model offers other categories as listed below:

Tag Questions

You can displace resistance from a statement by placing a question after the statement, can't you?

The question added at the end draws the conscious mind's attention thereby allowing the other information in the sentence to go directly into the unconscious mind.

"It is OK for me to do that, isn't it?"

Tag questions "tamp down" the suggestion
contained at the front part of the sentence into the
unconscious mind.

Examples:
Isn't it?
Have you?
You know?
Won't you?
Can't you?
Aren't you/we?
That's right?
Don't you know?
Didn't I?
Couldn't you?
Will you?
And you can, can you not?

Pacing Current Experience

A powerful means of building rapport and inducing
trance involves pacing the client's current
experience by simply making statements that
"agree with and have similarity with" their ongoing
experience.

Pacing current experience associates the person
into an internal focus.

"You can feel yourself sitting in your chair or lying down... And, as you listen to my voice, you continue to breathe in and out at first quickly and then as you take a deep breath you can become more relaxed, won't you, now? The sounds in the room and those that you may hear outside, means that you can go deeper and still deeper into trance."

Of course, noticing the sounds in the room has nothing to do with relaxation UNLESS you link the two.

Your subconscious mind could say, "Yes, now that you mention it, I do hear sounds and I can take a deep breath and of course, this makes the next statement about going into a trance much more believable."

Examples:
You hear my voice.
We are in this group.
You will enjoy it more.
As you notice each blink of your eyes.
As you sit here now you can hear external sounds.
...
And you can hear internal sounds...
You can experience being bathed by the light...
As you continue breathing in and out...
You can experience yourself going deeper and deeper into trance

Double Binds

"And you can go into a trance now or ten minutes from now and I don't know which you'll do ..."

If your unconscious mind accepted the presupposition of that sentence, you will either have already entered a trance or you will shortly.

Double binds have an unspoken presupposition contained within the sentence.

Vibrational Frequencies of POWER MIND
Parents seem to have a natural talent at communicating double binds. "John, when will you do your homework? Before this TV program comes on or as soon as it ends?"

"Now that you have entered a trance, which arm do you wish to lift?" "Do you wish for your right arm to raise or your left?" Asking which hand the image will come out on (in the Visual Squash) illustrates an example of a double bind.

Examples:
Do you want to begin now, or later?
As you dream, or upon awakening. ...
Either before, or after, leaving this room . . . .
When you go to bed you will either dream, or not.
Will you begin to change now or after this session?
Would you like to quit smoking today or tomorrow?

Would you like to buy the car now, or test drive it first?

You either will or you won't (followed by an unspecified verb).

Take all the time you need to finish up in the next five minutes.

You can change as quickly or as slowly as you want to now.

If you don't write at least one more double bind in the space below now, you will either think of one automatically very soon, or else wonder when the next one will come to mind, so you can write it down then.

Conversational Postulate

A conversational postulate takes the form of a "modal operator" question which is actually a command to do something.

The answer requires a yes or no response.

However, that question seems to bypass the conscious mind and create within the unconsciousness a desire to do something about the statement.

A classic example: "Can you close the door?" Instead of responding with a "yes" or "no," most of us respond by simply closing the door. Such questions avoid authoritarianism.

Examples:

Can you imagine this?
Will you just let go now?
Can you picture doing this?
Can you see what I am saying?
Can you reach that level now?
Would it be all right to feel this good?
Do you know that you know it already?
Could you open your mind for a moment?
How easily do you think you can do this?
Can you remember to be kind to yourself?
Does this sound like it will work for you?
Do you feel prepared to sign the contract now?
Do you think you can make the changes you want?
Would you like... to just sit here... and relax now?
Wouldn't you like to just drift into that peaceful state?
Would you mind writing down a couple more conversational postulates here?

Extended Quotes

Susan said that she heard Dave say that Tad James said, "I heard Richard say that NLP offers some of the most powerful, if not the most powerful, tools for personal change available today. And, these tools locate themselves within your unconscious mind.

In fact, you have access to them at the unconscious level. Once your conscious mind and unconscious mind gain rapport with each other then you will have total access to those resources."

Many speakers make extensive use of quotes.

The use of quotations takes the attention away from the speaker and serves to displace the conscious mind so the information can go into the unconscious mind.

The listener accesses a trance by focusing on the quotation as it facilitates an inward focus.

Extended quotes play off our need to make sense out of statements.

Examples:
Last year, I met a woman who said she knew a man who had mentioned that his father told him...
Andrew said that in a training four years ago, he had told the story about
When Richard Bandler was quoting Virginia Satir, who used to say that...
I was speaking with a friend the other day, who told me of a conversation she had had with a therapist who told her about a session he'd had with a client who said...
When I went to Brighton, East Sussex the other day with Kev and Julie, one of them told a story about when their mother would sit down and explain to the children how father had said...
The other day, a participant in the training told me that her husband said

Dick had told him to ask you to write a couple of
extended quotes down right here.

Selectional Restriction Violation

A selectional restriction violation describes an
ill-formed sentence which ascribes feelings to an
animal or some inanimate object.

"Have you ever thought about your pen, typewriter,
or word processor? Just think how many notes it
has taken over the years. How many, I wonder? It
knows more than even you know." "What about
giving your chair some thought?

Don't you know it gets tired? After all, it has
carried your weight for a long time, hasn't it?"

Examples:
My rock said...
The walls have ears.
That nail hurt my tire.
Flowers like to be picked.
My car knows how to get here.
Put the noise down in your toe.
What did your actions say to you?
Could you open your mind for a moment and just
listen to what the butterfly has to tell you?
Because the words have power of their own.
The cat doesn't care about the furniture's outrage
from the scratching.

As he picked up the spoon, the Jell-O trembled with fear.
And if your pen told us all the things it has learned.
My car loves to go fast when the road beckons.
Do trees cry when they drop their leaves?
Sometimes the cookies just call to you.
Do you know what the pen thought?
These walls can tell such stories.
Your pen knows how to write selectional restriction violations very easily, if you will just lead it to the lines below now.
In Handler's Weight Loss Transcript he utilizes the following Selectional
Restriction Violations:
The furnace inside you ..." This refers to the metabolism of the body.
I want to talk to that part of you... or you're unconscious."
And this is what he installs in people..."
And your brain goes brrrrrrr..."
The box of Godiva chocolates calls out to you."

Phonological Ambiguities

Many words have different meanings but sound the same. "Your nose/ knows the truth of this." "You can be hear/here anytime you wish."
Such language distracts the conscious mind. The client will go into trance while trying to sort out the ambiguities.

Examples:

you're/your
There/their
Here/hear
Son/sun
Bare/bear bottoms
There's no "their" in there
He reddened as he read in it.
You are the one who has won.
After all you have learned from the tapes.
And here today as you hear your unconscious mind
You can trust you're unconscious mind now

Syntactic Ambiguity

Syntactic ambiguity exists when we cannot
immediately determine from the immediate
context the function (syntactic) of a word.

For instance, "Hurting people can feel difficult."

Does that sentence mean that when you meet
hurting people they can make this difficult for us
emotionally or does it mean that engaging in the
behaviour of hurting people feels like a difficult
problem?

We can construct syntactic ambiguities by using a
verb plus "- ing."
Then you construct a sentence so that it lacks
clarity about whether the "-ing" word functions as
an adjective or as a verb.

Examples:
Running water
Shooting stars
Babbling brook
Hypnotizing hypnotists can be tricky

Scope Ambiguity

Scope ambiguity exists when you cannot determine by context how much one portion of a sentence applies to another portion.

"The organization consists of healthy men and women." Do we mean to imply that just the men have the quality of "health" or do we mean to include the women as healthy as well?

You can construct Scope Ambiguity by adding an "-ing" on a verb and put an "and" between the objects.

Example:
Your deep breathing and trance...
Hearing Bob and John...
Yesterday I was driving my car with tennis shoes on
I was riding my horse with blue jeans on.
10. Punctuation Ambiguity
There exist three kinds of punctuation ambiguities. The first involve run-on sentences. "I want you to notice your hand me the book." "On your arm I see

a watch yourself go into trance." The second form involves improper pauses.

This form of sentence involves times when you begin a.... uh... sentence and you never quite... uh... finish the... sentence.
This causes a forced mind reading and becomes highly trance inducing. Newscaster, Paul Harvey, does this in a marvellous way when he says, "... good... day."

The third type of punctuation ambiguity involves an incomplete sentence.

In this form you begin a sentence and you never quite... You then go on to another sentence with a totally different thought.

Examples (run-on sentences):
Let me take your hand me the pen.
See the butterfly drifting over the hilltop is a beautiful valley.
She has freckles on her butt I like her anyway.
Examples (improper pauses):
My wife left me... to go to Texas.
I was looking for my tie... into this thought.
If you hear any ambiguities, it's all right to write them right here

Utilization

Erickson utilized utilization to its fullest potential.
He used everything the client said.

He used every sound and incident in the room.

In one training a wall chart fell off the wall. Tad
James said, "And old concepts are falling away."

Once when I used hypnosis with a client, I had a
relaxation tape playing.

Suddenly the tape finished. I knew that in a short
moment that the tape player would make a click as
it cut off. So, I said, "In just a moment you will hear
a click. And, when you do, that means you will let
go of the pain totally and completely"

In a brief moment the player clicked and the
client's body jumped as the emotion totally
released.

Examples:
Client: "I don't think I know/"
Practitioner: "That's right, you don't think you
know.
Client: "I can't be hypnotized."
Practitioner: "That's right. You can't be hypnotized
yet.
Client: "I'm not sold."
Salesman: "That's right, because you haven't asked
the one question yet that will let you be sold."

Embedded Commands

Erickson worked as a master at giving the unconscious mind directions through embedded commands.

He would mark out such words that he wanted to go into the unconscious mind. To give such commands and mark out words, we have to both lower our tone and raise the volume of the voice. "It is possible for you to instruct a client's unconscious mind through embedded commands to get well, now."

Say, did you get the command from the marked out words? When you have a client dissociated above their Time-Line, this offers a wonderful opportunity to send embedded commands to the unconscious mind.

When using Time-Line processes, the client will have then entered into a rather deep trance.

Analogue Marking

Erickson would mark out the words that he wanted to go into the unconscious mind.

Marking out refers to emphasizing specific words or phrases by altering tonality.
POWER MIND KNOW THIS ALL THAT CRAP WAS NOT YOURS.

In giving these commands and marking out words, both lower your tone and raise the volume of your voice.

It is possible for you to instruct a client's unconscious mind through embedded commands to get well, now.

Did you get the command from the marked out words?

Spell Out Words

Spelling out key words we draw attention to the word we are spelling out. This induces trance. And, you k-n-o-w that spelling out words does induce trance, doesn't it?

Linkage Language

This refers to the verbal process of describing (pacing) observable and verifiable behaviour in the listener.

Then, by using a "linking word," the speaker goes on to describe (leading) the desired behaviour. Different people, of course, respond differently to each pattern.

Linkage language involves the process of utilization connected to specific linking words.

a. Conjunctions

Use a conjunction such as "and" to link observable behaviour and desired experience. The conjunction links the pacing statement to the leading statement. ("X" and "Y").

Example: "As you sit there, breathing and reading this document and you can begin to breathe more deeply and become more relaxed."

The purpose here involves linking the pacing statement to the leading statement so that the latter seems to follow logically from the former.

Thus, the linkage collapses information boundaries to enhance the sense of continuity. Additional pacing statements further enhances the effect ("X" and "X" and "X" and "Y").

Examples: "As you sit in your chair (pacing) and read this paper (pacing) and I communicate to you (pacing) and you can breathe deeply and relax more thoroughly (leading)."

b. Disjunction

Using the contrasting or negative form of conjunctions can also sometimes achieve the same results. ("X" and "X" and "X" but "Y").

Examples: "I don't know whether you prefer to continue gazing at this paper (pacing), or, whether you'd like to look elsewhere (pacing), or whether you'd like to breathe deeper (pacing), but I do know that your conscious can develop a trance that will fit nicely your present needs (leading)."

c. Adverbial Clauses or Implied Causatives

Causatives often exist as "time" words that imply that one event inevitably functions as linked in time with, or caused by the other.

Key implied Causatives include:

(1) Since "X" then "Y." Since you are now breathing deeper, you can begin to relax even more.

(2) When "X" then "Y." When you settle comfortably into that chair, you can allow your eyes to slowly close.

(3)While "X" then "Y" While you remember that very special time and place, you can comfortably begin to develop that trance.

(4) After "X" then "Y" After you have become very comfortable, you can begin to allow your trance to develop.

(5) Other implied causatives words include: often, as, before, during, following and throughout.

To familiarize yourself with these language patterns, write down five sentences for each.

Include the Meta-Model violations as well in your exercise.

You will find these skills most helpful in all areas of communication and highly useful in public speaking.

"Hypnosis" and trance describes nothing new, odd, occult, strange or mysterious.

Our consciousness can "come up" (uptime) and "go down" (downtime).

And when it goes down inside—we enter into another world, the inner world of meaning, belief, concepts—a world of spirit where we create our neuro-semantic reality.

Nor can we escape from this. We can only effectively develop awareness and understanding of this and how it plays out in communication in everyday life so that we can have more choice and control over it. When we do that, then we can choose our hypnotists well.

Then we can know when to "go into trance" and when to come out!

Then we will not allow ourselves to unknowingly or unconsciously receive the onslaught of the bad suggestions that some people forever put out. Then we can know how to dehypnotize ourselves from the dysfunctional negative suggestions left over (in our heads) from childhood.

Then we can take a proactive stance in communicating positive and enhancing suggestions for ourselves and others.

This empowers us in communicating professionally and consciously.

Milton Model Language Patterns Using Meta-Model Violations

1. Mind Reading – Modal Operators of Possibility
2. Lost Performative – Nominalizations
3. Cause-Effect – Unspecified Verbs
4. Complex Equivalence – Simple Deletions
5. Presuppositions – Lack of Referential Index
6. Universal Quantifiers – Comparative Deletions

Steps in Communicating

1. Determine your Well-Formed Outcome
2. Build rapport and test
3. Gather information with the Meta-Model
4. Use Milton Model language patterns to:

a) Induce trance.
b) Directionalize language towards outcome.
c) Deliver embedded commands toward outcome

Anchoring

An Anchor is any stimulus that triggers a state (a state is a representation or series of representations).

When an anchor is "fired off", it will allow you to get all or part of the feelings back from a particular experience.

Anchors can be naturally occurring, or you can deliberately set an anchor for yourself or others.

All experience is coded in the mind as a gestalt of sensory information in all systems (Visual, Auditory, or Kinesthetic).

Whenever any component of a particular experience is "triggered" in any system, other components of that experience will be re-accessed to some degree.

Therefore, any part of the experience can be used to access another part of the experience.

<u>Naturally occurring anchors</u>

Some examples of naturally occurring anchors:

- Your country's national anthem being sung/played

- Some habit of your spouse that elicits a less-than-glorious state in you, like leaving toilet seat up/toothpaste lid off.

- Hearing someone you care for saying "I love you."

- Holiday snaps

- A certain look from a partner or parent that indicates you are in trouble

- The smell of spring rain, freshly mown grass, bonfires etc

Most of us have had the experience, in communicating with a client, friend or associate, of reaching a certain level of Rapport and understanding that was a very positive resource for both of you.

Later on, the flow of the conversation, discussion or negotiation changes.

The interaction becomes more tense, strained or difficult and you wish you had a way of re-accessing the positive experiences that you shared earlier.

Anchoring is a process that allows you to do this.

Examples of deliberately anchoring

- Touch yourself or other person in a specific place for a specific length of time (knee, shoulder, arm, hands, etc.)

- Use a unique handshake (e.g. Touch their shoulder when you shake hands) "Mark out" words you speak with a tonal shift (called analogue marking)

- Raise your eyebrows every time your subject does what you want to anchor Use a unique gesture. Spatial

In each of these something elicited memories, feelings and behaviour.

This stimulus-response reaction goes back to the early Russian psychologist, Ivan Pavlov, and his experiments with unconditioned and conditioned responses.

As Pavlov studied dogs, he discovered that they would salivate upon seeing, smelling, and tasting meat.

He added the sound of a bell or a tuning fork when he gave the dogs the meat.

After a few repetitions of conditioning, he would only sound the bell or tuning fork to elicit their salivation response.

This became foundational in behavioural psychology and learning theory.

Anchoring is the NLP user-friendly form of Pavlovian conditioning.

In NLP, anchoring refers to the natural process by which any element of an experience (any sensory modality component) can recreate (re-evoke) the entire experience.

And, inasmuch as individual skills result from the development and sequencing of rep systems, stimuli that evoke any part of the representation will often trigger the entire experience. Actually, we inevitably set and fire off anchors all the time.

One cannot live without doing so. NLP simply makes us aware of the process.

Knowing the neuro- linguistic process of anchoring explains how "first impressions form lasting impressions."

First anchors last because they set the frame. Awareness of setting anchors in others and ourselves gives us the ability to control the process.

We can then set anchors that serve ourselves and others well, bring out our best, and create a context for openness and learning.

Every time we communicate or send messages, we anchor representations.

We use words (sound and/or visual symbols—signals) to represent something else and to evoke thoughts, representations, ideas, memories, values, etc. Sensory-based words quickly elicit their referents.

Remember anchors are present within all of us as they are naturally occurring.

When you read the following phrases what do you think of?

- I'm loving it!
- It's the real thing
- Ver sprung durch technik

These are all phrases used by advertisers and they are designed to both elicit responses in making us remember who the advert is for in relation to brand and product.

Negative as well as positive anchors can occur, maybe you had your heart broken to a particular love song, or a certain smell makes you homesick etc.

These anchors can be intensified by life experience and negative anchors can be debilitating sometimes so it is of benefit to be able to rid ourselves of them.

By using our mind intentionally we can do just that.
We inevitably set and fire off anchors all the time. One cannot live without doing so.

NLP simply makes us aware of the process. Knowing the neuro- linguistic process of anchoring explains how "first impressions form lasting impressions."

First anchors last because they set the frame.
Awareness of setting anchors in others and
ourselves gives us the ability to control the process.
We can then set anchors that serve ourselves and
others well, bring out our best, and create a
context for openness and learning.

Important things to remember about Anchoring

1. Anchors do not need to be conditioned over long
periods of time in order to become established.

Repeated stimuli can reinforce an Anchor, but
Anchors tend to promote the use of single trial
learning.

2. Anchors will become established without direct
rewards or reinforcements for the association.

Repetition and conditioning can lead to the
establishment of an Anchor, but they are not
necessary.

3. Internal experience (cognitive behaviour) is
considered to be as significant as overt measurable
response. In other words, NLP asserts that an
internal picture, feeling, or dialogue is just as much
a response as the saliva of Pavlov's dog.

4. The more intense the experience the individual
is having at the time the Anchor is "set" (the

stimulus applied), the stronger the response will be when the Anchor is "fired off" (re-introduced) at a later time. Phobias are an example of powerful Anchors that, in most cases, are established in a single, very brief and intense learning experience.

5. When eliciting a state you wish to Anchor, be sure the person has a specific example, a single event when that state was paramount. The memory of the experience should be associated.

That is, the person should remember the event as if it were happening now, seeing what they saw, hearing what they heard and feeling what they were feeling.

6. In creating an anchor, precise timing of the trigger stimulus is critical.

In eliciting a state from someone, (asking them to think of a person they like, for instance), the state reaches full intensity rather quickly and then diminishes slowly.

Notice the physiological changes the person goes through as they remember the event, set and release your anchor just before the experience peaks.

Note: You can use the person's first memory of the experience to calibrate their physiology so you know what they look like when the experience peaks.

Then have them repeat the memory; this time set the anchor.

7. The more unique the stimuli (anchor) the more accurate it will be in re- accessing the desired state.

In other words, the anchor will be less likely to bring with it any unwanted representations which had similar associations.

8. The more accurately the stimulus is replicated, the quicker and more accurately it will re-access what was associated with it originally.

9. When you test your Anchor, if you do not see the same physical response

- The Anchor was set too late (when the state was diminishing)
- Firing the Anchor did not precisely replicate the "set"

10. Anchors can be established in any of the Representational Systems.

Often, the most powerful Anchor is in the sensory system the person is least aware of.

If you anchor in multiple systems (for example, touching a knee while making a sound, "shoop"), it will be more powerful than using only one system.

11. Anchors can be set and fired off covertly or overtly.

The fact of everyday living is that people are constantly creating and utilizing powerful Anchors covertly and most of the time doing so outside of their own conscious awareness.

An exciting outcome of your training will be to gain more control of the Anchoring you do naturally, so you can produce the responses you want in others and in yourself.

Metaphors

The major purpose of a metaphor is to pace and lead a client's behaviour through a story.

The major points of construction consist of

1. Displacing the referential index from the client to a character in a story.
2. Pacing the client's problem by establishing behaviours and events between the characters in the story that are similar to those in the client's situation.
3. Accessing resources for the client within the context of the story, Finishing the story such that a sequence of events occurs in which the characters in the story resolve the conflict and achieve the desired outcome.

The basic steps to generate a metaphor are:

Pre Mapping

Identify the sequence of behaviour and/or events in question: this could range from a conflict between internal parts, to a physical illness, to problematic interrelationships between the client and parents, a boss or a spouse.

Strategy analysis

Is there any consistent sequence of representations contributing to the current behavioural outcome?

Identify the desired new outcomes and choices

This may be done at any level of detail, and is important that you have an outcome to work for.

Establish anchors

For strategic elements involved in this current behaviour and the desired outcome.

For instance, in one knee you might anchor all of the strategies and representations that stop the client from having the necessary choices; and on the other knee you might anchor any personal resources (regardless of specific contexts) that the client may have.

Mapping Strategies

Displace referential indices: map over all nouns (objects and elements) to establish the characters in the story.

The characters may be anything, animate or inanimate, from rocks to forest creatures to cowboys to books, etc.

What you choose as characters is not important so long as you preserve the character relationship. Very often you may want to use characters from well-known fairy tales and myths.

Establish an isomorphism

Between the client's situation and behaviour, and
the situation and behaviours of the characters in
the story - map over all verbs (relations and
interactions)

Assign behavioural traits, such as strategies and
representational characteristics, that parallel those
in the client's present situation (i.e., pace the
client's situation with the story).

Make use of any anchors you have established
previously to secure the relationship.

Access and establish new resources

In terms of the characters and events in the story:
This may be done within the framework of a
Reframing or re- accessing of a forgotten resource;
again, using any appropriate pre- established
anchors.

You may choose to keep the actual content of the
resource ambiguous allowing the client's
unconscious processes to choose the appropriate
one.

Use nonsequiturs, ambiguities and direct quotes

To break up sequences in the story and direct
conscious resistance, if such resistance is present

and is hindering the effect of the metaphor. Conscious understanding does not, of course, necessarily interfere with the metaphoric process.

Keep your resolution as ambiguous as necessary

To allow the client's unconscious processes to make the appropriate changes.

Collapse the pre- established anchors and provide a future pace, if possible, to check your work.

Modelling

The basis of NLP is the Process of Modelling, which has three elements

1. Belief & Values Systems
2. Physiology
3. Strategies

The theory is that, "Anything you can do, I can elicit and also do."

Through the process of Modelling, you can find and model excellent behaviour and install it in someone else.

In successful people we often observe that they are generally in control of their state no matter what the external circumstances, and that they have a most excellent way of staying in a positive frame of mind.

NLP modelling is at the very heart of NLP.

NLP aims to discover how experts or superior performers excel in every and any given niche.

This it is asserted can be achieved through a careful process of reductive observation and imitation; the idea being that the core skills – the difference that makes the difference - can be identified, isolated, coded and "run" to produce excellence to order.

Basically if one person can achieve something then anyone can learn to achieve it.

Act "as if" by replicating their internal model and eliciting their strategy and you will achieve the same or similar outcome.

Successful Modelling

A classic example in NLP is the spelling strategy.

Robert Dilts (1997), among others, claims that the inability to spell is usually not a matter of a person being unintelligent, but of using an inappropriate strategy.

From repeated observation (particularly of eye accessing cues), successful spellers access an internal visual image of the word they are spelling, then experience a felt response that the spelling is correct.

While this is embellished and varied according to the individual, the essence of the strategy can be learnt by those who have been ineffective at spelling.

A modelling project in NLP will codify many other aspects of experience besides the mental strategy, such as language patterns, beliefs, and more.

In itself, modelling excellence can be remarkably simple.
Theoretically, it just involves looking at what it is high achievers and performers do and say, and doing the same.

The hard bit of course is trying to actively discern the little differences that make the difference.

In a nut shell then, modelling is essentially about detecting and codifying the little differences –the nuances - that effect (bring about) successful states of being [be they psychological, physiological or socio-cultural] in otherwise normal human beings.

The three filters

The first filter is values and Beliefs.

They are essentially an evaluation filter.

They are how we decide whether our actions are good or bad, or right or wrong.

Values

And they are how we decide about how we feel about our actions. Values are arranged in a hierarchy with the most important one typically being at the top and lesser ones below that.

We all have different models of world (an internal model about the world), and our values are the result of our model of the world.

When we communicate with ourselves or someone else, if our model of the world conflicts with our values or their values, then there's going to be a conflict. Richard Bandler says, "Values are those things we don't live up to."

Values are what people typically move toward or away from (see Meta Programs). They are our attractions or repulsions in life. They are essentially a deep, unconscious belief system about what's important and what's good or bad to us. Values change with context too.

That is, you probably have certain values about what you want in a relationship and what you want in business. Your values about what you want in one and in the other may be quite different. And actually, if they're not, it's possible that you may have trouble with both. Since values are context related, they may also be state related, although values are definitely less related to state than are beliefs.

Beliefs

Beliefs are generalizations about how the world is.

One of the important elements in modelling is to find a person's beliefs about the particular behaviour we are trying to model.

Richard Bandler says "Beliefs are those things we can't get around."

Beliefs are the presuppositions that we have about the way the world is that either create or deny personal power to us.

So, beliefs are essentially our on/off switch for our ability to do anything in the world.

In the process of working with someone's beliefs, it's important to elicit or find out what beliefs they have that cause them to do what they do. We also want to find out the dis-enabling beliefs, the ones that do not allow them to do what they want to do.

The NLP model arose originally as an experiment in modelling examples of human excellence.

The second filter is the Physiology.

Physiology

These all refer to a single notion of internal strategies being visual, auditory, or kinesthetic (with a less likely extra olfactory and gustatory).

1. Body posture

2. Breathing
3. Gestures towards eyes ears or body
4. Eye movements (See PRS)
5. Language patterns (meta-model) and predicates   such as "I see!" "Sounds right! Or "I feel that..."

And finally

<u>Strategies</u>

What they are and how to work with them.

We describe these processes and learning's as strategies.

As we "run our brain" and nervous system in structured and organized ways, deleting, generalizing, distorting, etc., our brain gets into the habit of "going to the same place."

It develops a strategy or sequence of rep systems to generate its experiences.

For this reason we say that every experience has an internal structure.

Even disorganized states such as madness, confusion, stress, procrastination, etc., have a governing, specific, sensory blueprint.

Strategies simply provide a formal description of what we do inside our head and nervous system to generate some particular behaviour, whether it consist of thoughts, emotions, beliefs, values, states, skills, experiences, communication, etc.

All behaviour (learning, remembering, motivation, making a choice, communicating, changing, etc.) results from systematically ordered sequences of sensory representations.

Strategies – The Components

Discover: The first step is to discover the person's strategy through the process of elicitation.

Utilization: The next step is to utilize the strategy by feeding back information to the person in the order and sequence that it was elicited.

Change & Design: The next step is to then be able to change the strategy –to make changes in it so that it produces the desired outcome. This component includes the design of strategies.

Installation: We then may want to install a new strategy if needed.

Everything We Do: Strategies involve everything we do. All our daily activity is generated & maintained by strategies.

Whether or not we finish what we do is governed by a strategy.

Components:

- Visual –External Internal Constructed Remembered

- Auditory – External Internal Constructed Remembered

- Auditory Digital

- Kinesthetic – External Internal Constructed Remembered Proprioceptive

- Tactile Meta

- Olfactory – External Internal Constructed Remembered

- Gustatory – External Internal Constructed Remembered

The TOTE model

Presupposes that we can achieve behavioural excellence through having:

1. A future goal in mind

2. Sensory and behavioural evidence that in dictates the achieving of the goal

3. A range of operations, procedures or choices with which to accomplish the goal.

Designating this process a mental strategy, Dilts, Bandler, Grinder, and DeLozier (1980) articulated the NLP model with the template of the TOTE.

As they did this they enriched and extended the TOTE to include the pieces of subjectivity that they discovered: sensory rep system, Submodalities, eye accessing cues, and linguistic predicates, etc.

By these pieces one could unpack an unconscious strategy, anchor the elements together, and reframe its meanings, and thereby design and install a strategy.

They thought that this would provide a fully articulated model for modelling excellence.

The TOTE model is a planning tool.

T = Test
O = Operate
T = Test
E = Exit

For this model to be valid we have to accept that the stimulus behind behaviour is the achievement of a Goal.

In order to achieve the Goal, that goal has to be defined thoroughly enough to allow us to recognise when the goal has been achieved so that as we move towards the achievement of that goal (operate) we can assess (test) if that goal has been achieved and then Exit.

To identify strategies we need the ability to:

- Identify the strategy
- Elicit the strategy
- Interrupt or alter the strategy
- Design new strategies or redesign old ones
- Install the strategy, or utilize it in a different context.

These skills also presuppose awareness and sensitivity to the signs and cues that indicate the operation of a strategy.

We need to be skilful in managing the strategy that we elicit via anchoring, reframing, pacing, etc.

We need to be able to compare and analyze between strategies in order to improve their design.

Strategy Elicitation

When we want the recipe for a delicious dish and how to cook, we need specific information about the elements, their amounts, the order, etc.

The same holds with getting the structure of subjective experiences.
1) Establish a positive frame for rapport. "You do that very well; teach me how to do that." "Suppose I lived your life for a day, how would I do this?"

2) Access the state. The person needs to associate fully and congruently with the skill or state. To fully elicit their strategy, take the person back to the place where the behaviour naturally occurs.

This lets the context; with its natural anchors (sitting at a keyboard) elicit the response.

Or we can elicit the state by reproducing a portion of the context (tonality, gestures, play-acting, etc.).

3) Intensify the state.

In elicitation, the more of the state we evoke, the better.

4) Explore the "how/ "How do you make this?"

If the person has consciousness of their strategy, they will tell you.

If not, expect them to demonstrate it.

Eliciting involves good questioning techniques that evokes a person to carry out a task that requires the strategy.

"Have you ever experienced a time when you really felt motivated to do something?
"When did that last occur when you felt really motivated?"

"What does that feel like when you felt exceptionally creative?"

"Have you ever gotten into a situation where you felt very creative?"

Accessing questions involve a person recalling an experience.

"What did it feel like?"

"How did you do it?"

"When do you feel best able to do it?"

"What do you need to do it?"

"What happens as you do it?"

"When did that last occur?"

Such questions encourage a person to "go inside" to their memory banks and access their personal history.

Doing this Trans-derivational Search (TDS) to our reference experiences not only serves as the way we all make sense of things and deal with stimuli, but also how we use such to re-create states and experience.
We can also use this TDS process to assist someone to go back through "time" to recover the full experience.

5) Calibrate from an uptime state.

Being fully alert and open to the person's external cues enables us to calibrate to the state as we watch the person demonstrate the strategy People typically demonstrate as they talk about problems, outcomes, or experiences (the mind-body systemic response).

Our attentiveness to such "instant replays" enables us to note how they cycle through the sequence of representations that lead to their response.

6) Ask them to exaggerate. If we don't get the strategy, invite the person to exaggerate some small portion of the strategy. Exaggerating one

step in a strategy may also access other representations linked to it synesthetically

7) Stay Meta to the content.

Remember that strategies operate as purely formal structures.

In NLP we typically focus on eliciting excellence rather than pathology in human experience. We elicit resourceful experiences (creativity, motivation, remembering, decision, conviction, confidence, etc.). This is what you say:
"As you remember a time when you experienced all your full resources and potential as a person, go back to that occasion, now, so that you re-experience that event fully and completely"

General and basic elicitation question include:
Trigger questions:

"How do you know when to begin the process of...?" (motivation, deciding, learning)

"What lets you know you feel ready to...?"

Operation questions:

"What do you do first?"

"What happens as you begin?"

"What do you do when you don't feel sure that you have reached your goal?"

Test questions:

"What comparisons do you make?

"How do you know that you have satisfied your criteria?"

Choice point questions:

"What lets you know you have finished?"
"What lets you know you should move on to something else?"

"What lets you know you have not succeeded at this?"

"How do you know you've ended your process?"
If we think about the learning strategy, then once we ask a person to think about a time or situation wherein they learned something extremely well with ease and competence and then we can ask the following:

Operations questions:

"What happens as you learn something?"

"What do you do as you prepare to learn something?"

"What steps do you go through to learn something quickly?"

"What do you do when you don't feel sure that you have met your criteria?"

Test questions:

"What demonstrates that you have successfully learned something quickly?"

"How do you know when you have learned something quickly?"

"How do you test whether you have achieved your desired outcome?"

Decision Point questions:

"How do you know when you have successfully learned easily and effectively?"

"What lets you know that you have not yet finished learning something?"

"What lets you know that you feel ready to move on to something else?"

"When you don't feel sure you have successfully learned something, what lets you know that?"

Suppose we want to track the brain-body (neuro-linguistics) of someone who completes a task generally considered unpleasant and discover their strategy.

Begin by asking generally, "How do you get yourself to do an unpleasant task like cleaning the toilet, taking out the garbage, doing taxes, etc."

Then invite them to access that state. "Think of a time when you motivated yourself to do something that you didn't want to do.

How did you do that? What pictures, voices, and messages, etc., did you use to motivate yourself to do something you found unpleasant?"

One man interviewed would look at the situation externally and make a constructed image of seeing himself carrying out the proposed behaviour and then quickly fast-forward the movie to the end where he sees the desired results.

He would get a positive feeling of muscle tension and increasing warmth as he watched this internal movie.

He would then hear a voice saying, "Just do it" in a matter-of-fact tonality. When he heard that voice, he would simply rise and execute the behaviour.

Unpacking Strategies (At speed)

One problem involved in unpacking strategies that we want to model, modify, or utilize—they zoom by!

So how can we identify the appropriate steps in the sequence if they go so fast? This holds especially true for those that have achieved the status of an unconscious TOTE.

To identify each step we must either increase our abilities to observe rapid and minute behavioural changes or slow the process down by asking good questions.
"What happened first that allowed you to respond so creatively in that situation?"

"What do you do first when you motivate yourself?"

Keep asking until you find the initial external stimulus that triggers the strategy.
"What happens just before that?"

1) Unpack strategies in terms of predicates.

We tend to reveal our preferred rep system (seeing, hearing, feeling, etc) in the kind of language predicates we use.

These predicate words are adjectives, verbs, adverbs and other descriptive words that identify what we assert (or predicate).

We can also listen for predicate combinations indicating Synesthesia patterns.

"That looks uncomfortable" (V–K)

"It sounds like colourful place" (A–V)

"Don't look at me with that tone of voice" (V–A)

"It sounded frightening" (A–K)
By going Meta to this content we can note its form and structure.

2) Unpack strategies in terms of accessing cues.

Most of our communication takes place on the unconscious level.

We are usually unaware of the vast majority of representations that pass through our neurological systems as we cycle through our strategies.
Yet all behaviour indicates our internal neurological processes and therefore carries information about them.

We are able to decode this form of communication as we gather information.

3) Unpack by asking logical questions.

Does the strategy make logical sense?

If a person seems to jump steps in the process, ask backing-up questions to get to the beginning of the strategy.

"What happened first that allowed you to feel motivated in that situation?"

Back up. "What did you do before that?"
"What stimulated that?"

Eventually we find the initial external stimulus that triggered the strategy and thus the step-by-step process.

4) Unpack using the Strategy Notational System.

"I hear alarm clock, then look at it as I turn it off. Then I lie down again and feel how comfortable bed is. Eventually an internal voice says, 'If you stay here, you'll go to sleep and be late/ so I make a picture of a time when I was late for work. I then feel bad and I say to myself, 'It will be worse next time/ and make a bigger picture of what will happen if late again and feel worse.

When the bad feeling is strong enough, I get up."

Then we notate it as follows:

Ae » Ve » Ke+i » Aid » V1^ » K1- (loop) » Exit

Loop back
"I picture all the things that I am going to do during
the day and feel good about them. The pleasant
pictures then 'pulls me out of bed/ If have to do
something unpleasant, I think about how
wonderful it will be when it is done/"

Vi+/Vi+/Vi+ » Ki+ » Aid-+ -» Exit

"I feel a sensation of warmth and say to myself, 'I
have to get up/ this voice is in a calm, easy tone. As
voice speeds up, it becomes more clear and
distinct, and I become more alert."
Ki+ » Aitd/Aitd/ » Exit

(Analogue increase in volume/pitch)

Designing Strategies

Some strategies just don't work very well or could
work a lot better if streamlined in some way, or if
we added additional resources.

Many times we can redesign better tests and
operations in our strategies by simply making sure
that we have all of the rep system components
represented.

What do you hear around you?
What does it sound like?

195

What do you hear inside your head?
What do you see around you?
Describe the tone in your internal dialogue...
What internal pictures do you see?
How do you feel internally?
What qualities do these pictures have?
What do you smell?
What body awareness do you have tactilely or externally?
What tastes do you experience in this?

Strategizing involves sending the brain in productive directions. It describes the process of organizing representational components in certain sequences to create the desired outcome.

This skill is more important than intelligence in achieving outcomes.

We can learn about our styles of thinking and responding by becoming aware the steps in our strategies that lie between the original stimulus and the resulting behaviour.

Then we will have more choices about how to respond and how to change a strategy program.

Designing New and Better Strategies

The strategy model enables us to actually design custom-made strategies for achieving specific outcomes.

In strategy design we create desired outcomes, trouble-shoot problems, streamline cumbersome and inefficient strategies, limit strategies that we use too generally, re-contextualize others to appropriate contexts, install appropriate tests, etc.

We need to have well-formed strategies.

For example: making sure that we have all the necessary tests and operations.
When we use strategies for modelling, we find someone who already has the ability to achieve the outcome and simply identify and use that strategy as a model.

If a person has a good strategy for reading and criticizing literature, but not for generating it, we don't want to model that for creating literature.

When we tailor a strategy for a specific task and person, we must first determine the kinds of discriminations we need.

Which rep system will we need for gathering information?

Do we have the needed rep system?

Do we need to break a synesthesia pattern or divert it so it doesn't interfere?

How much rehearsal will we need to practice with the new sequence?

<u>A well-formed strategy involves knowing</u>

The kind of information (for input, feedback) that we need and in which rep system.

1. What kind of tests, distinctions, generalizations, associations we need to make in processing that information.

2. What specific operations and outputs we need to achieve the outcome.

3. The most efficient and effective sequence for testing and operating.

4. An explicit representation of the designed outcome. Without specifically identifying an outcome when we "operate" and compare the representation of present state with desired state, the strategy will break down.

This explains our need for representations of the outcome.

"What do you want?"

"How will you know if you've changed...?"
"If you have designed an ecological strategy."

"Will this violate personal or organizational ecology?"

We make sure the strategy doesn't conflict with other strategies.

In so working with human subjectivity, we will want to discover what "important reasons why" a person hasn't yet achieve an outcome.

The person's Meta- outcomes provide their behaviour in terms of some general goals (preservation, survival, growth, protection, betterment, adaptation).

If you have utilized the Visual, Auditory and Kinesthetic components of the rep system and if you have utilized both an internal and an external check, using all the rep systems, this will reduce the probability of looping, for example, getting stuck with no way of exiting.

Utilizing Strategies

The meaning of an experience depends partly on our outcome within a given context.

If we can use our creativity to transform obstacles into resources, we thereby expand our choices and behavioural repertoire.

One major use of strategy work is with modelling someone's language strategies.

This means that we have to unpack a sequence of thinking, deciding, or perceiving, etc., into steps using rep systems. If we then use that same sequence back to them, we will automatically be pacing them. We are thus developing such a strong rapport that they will find it difficult to resist our communication.

For example, if we notice that someone has a decision-making strategy that involves seeing then talking to themselves about it until it creates certain feelings (V —> Aid —> K$_1$ —> Exit) then we could use that sequence to organize our communication to them.

Doing this matches their form. We ask the person to picture clearly our idea, suggest some internal talk, and some feelings that this will likely generate.

We can also pace non-verbally by directing.

By so packaging our information so that it mirrors the individual's thinking processes, we make our communications maximally congruent to the person's model of the world.

If people cannot but respond to their own internal processes, then entering their world, identifying their strategies for buying, deciding, feeling motivated, feeling resourceful, acting in a pro-active way, etc., increases our effectiveness.

It assists in managing, communicating, relating, understanding, etc.

We no longer have to move through the world assuming or imposing our strategies for motivation, decision, belief, etc., on others. Once we have discovered their preferences we can fit our communication to their model.

We will become much more effective in understanding how to help the client make the changes they desire.

To motivate another, we find and use the person's motivational strategy.

To communicate, we find their strategy for understanding.

To manage, we find their strategy for trust.

To sell, we find their strategy for decision, valuing, planning, etc.

Installation of Strategies

We can install a strategy by anchoring, by rehearsing strategy pieces (new dialogue lines, gestures, facial expressions, etc.)/ by vicarious experiences (role-play), and by creating altered states and experiences.

By installing we get the strategy to function naturally and automatically, as an intact unit (a chunk) so that each step automatically ties into the next.

Installing through anchoring

Involves anchoring a representation or state and inserting the steps of the strategy as the person rehearses the strategy sequence.

Anchoring helps us "walk" a person through it.

When we anchor a sequence, we wire it to some contextual stimuli.

Elicit the steps of the strategy through questioning and observation and then anchor each step with the same anchor.

For example, we have someone access their motivation strategy.

"Think of a time when you felt really motivated..."
and then anchor that experience.

Later, we can fire off that anchor in a new context
so the person re-accesses that strategy sequence
for motivation in that new context.

Synesthesia patterns automatically carry through
on their own processes once initiated.

For example: a person with a phobia of water can
see a body of water and immediately have a phobic
reaction.

They see (Ve) water and feel (K1) fear.

We symbolize that phobia as Ve/K!.

A synesthesia has two component rep systems with
the first rep system triggering immediately the
second rep system.

We anchor these synesthesias and then tie them
into other situations.

This can streamline an inappropriately long
strategy and thereby avoid loops.

One man had a cumbersome and inefficient
decision-making strategy.

He would spend days in deliberation and put off decisions until he had passed up key opportunities.

Then he would feel agitated and angry with himself for wasting so much time.

In redesigning the strategy, he considered "the possibility of missing opportunities and wasting time" (Ad/K~) at an earlier point.
The question, "What does it feel like at the end of your strategy when you realized the value of wasted time and missed opportunities?" helped him install it.

This streamlined his strategy as it provided the needed motivation to decide earlier.

He used it as a resource by checking his time schedule and using his negative feelings as a decision point.

Instructions create new representational steps to install a new strategy

Since words work as anchors and can anchor a new strategy, we can install a strategy by "giving instructions."

A hands-on approach to installing a strategy is to rehearse the new way of doing things.

Simply ask someone to practice each representational step until they feel comfortable with it.

To develop the visual system, we can practice holding up an image, making mental snapshot of it, then closing our eyes and seeing it inside, etc.

Eventually we will develop the ability to create and hold an internal visual image in our mind's eye.

Game-playing rehearsal

By making a "game" of reading words in the air, this puts more emphasis on the form than on the content, or their past negative experiences.

Have the person learn where to look, where to put their head and eyes, when to use feelings, when to use pictures, etc.

By framing the process as a game, the rehearsal can feel more like dancing and playing than learning, spelling, or whatever.

Typically this makes the learning easier and less stressful.

Rehearsing synesthesia patterns

Offers another powerful method for installing sequences of rep systems independent of content.

Certain synesthesia patterns will feel unfamiliar and underdeveloped.

A/K: As you listen to the words in your head, pay attention to any body sensations that occur. Identify one set, then listen to the words again and allow another feeling to emerge.

Continue doing this until you have seven different feelings.
K/A: Pick the feeling most appropriate to the words pronounced internally and from that feeling generate seven sounds.

"Get in touch with that feeling and allow it to turn into a sound."

Pick one of the sounds, and let it generate an internal visual image.

We can install via overlapping accessing cues. V-K overlap: "Look down and to the right, defocus your eyes, breathe high, and shallow, and now create picture."

Repeat this process until the transition feels smooth and easy, and then anchor it.

Interrupting strategies

Sometimes we have to interrupt a strategy that has a well-beaten or ingrained path.

We can interrupt by overloading— by giving them more information than they can handle.

A naturally occurring overload is a noisy place where we "can't hear ourselves think."

In the same way that a person may feel so good (or bad) that they don't know what to do or say, as when they are overcome by an emotion, so they can be "overwhelmed by beauty/" or "knocked out" by smell.

Overloading interrupts their strategy, thereby preventing it from completing its cycle.

We interrupt or divert a strategy some input to shift the representational sequence away from the habitual sequence.

When lost in thought and noise overrides sequence and draws us away.

Stopping or blocking accessing cues provides a direct and powerful way of interrupting strategy (i.e. like waving hands in front of someone's face while they attempt to visualize!).

You can typically interrupt a depressive strategy by asking the person feeling depressed to sit up straight, hold their head up high, to take in a full breath, to throw their shoulders back, to open their eyes wide and to smile.

The typical depressive posture and breathing pattern tends to perpetuate the feeling of depression.

If they are slumped over, their head is accessing the kinesthetic, thereby preventing them from seeing or talking themselves into a better state! We may also spin out a strategy.

We do this by feeding the output of the strategy back into the strategy.

Strategy Elicitation

1. Get yourself into an uptime state.

2. Establish rapport.

3. Identify the strategy you wish to work with.

4. Help the person back into the experience (fully associated and congruent. Anchor the state. Speak in present time to maintain the state.)

5. Write down the steps you observe in proper sequence.

5. Notice all accessing cues to track the process of the strategy (Maintain alertness to eye movements, auditory markings, breathing patterns, gestures, etc.).

7. Backtrack when necessary to get to previous steps.

8. Ask basic questions: "How do you?" (decide, motivate, etc.). Know when it's time to start?
"And then?"
"What happens just before that?"
"How do you know what to do next?"
"How do you know you have finished?
"Teach me to do it like you do."
9. Check to see if the evolving sequence flows logically

10. Make sure you elicit and not install each stage. (Use neutral predicates.)

11. Make sure the person answers the question you ask.

12. Get as much detail as you need.

13. Watch for loops (recurring sequences that do not make progress).

14. Ask for the same strategy in a different context and check for duplication of the new sequence.

Example: Eliciting Decision Strategy

1. Re-experience a time when you made a good decision easily.

2. Imagine some future time or likely situation in which you need to make a strong decision. What would you do?

3. What takes place (what happens) when you decide something?

Test Questions:

1. Where did you first think about deciding?
2. How do you know when to decide?
3. What first thing lets you know to begin deciding? Warning: If you ask, "What do you see when you begin?" You may install a strategy rather than eliciting it.
3. What's the first thing you must do in order to decide something?

Operate Questions:

1. What do you do when you prepare to decide something?
2. How do you know it's time to try alternatives?
3. How do you know you have several options?
4. How do you generate alternatives?

5. What steps do you go through to decide something?

Test Questions:

1. How do you know when you have decided something? What criteria do you use in deciding?
2. How do you test your alternatives?
3. How do you know you prefer one option more than another?
4. What do you have to satisfy for you to know you have the right alternative and the time to decide?

Exit Questions:

1. What lets you know when you when you haven't yet finished deciding?
2. How do you know when you've made your choice?
3. How do you know you've decided?
4. What lets you know you have successfully decided?

Potential Problems People May Have With Their Decision Strategy

1. Problems knowing the time has arrived to decide:

   a) Not enough internal dialogue saying, "This isn't working."

b) Not enough pictures of current situation, pictures "fuzzy", or picture of the "road forking," etc.
c) Internal negative K (feeling badly about current problem, or not enough association).

2. Problems generating alternatives:

a) No visual construct.
b) Constructing options but not visualizing outcomes with them
c) Not enough options to choose from (too much "this or that").

3. Problems evaluating alternatives:

a) Options not represented in all systems, which makes evaluation difficult.
b) No external checks to get necessary data. (Others' responses, etc.)
c) Not enough data gathered to make good decisions.
d) Criteria not appropriate to context or not prioritized.
e) Inappropriate or irrelevant criteria chosen for making the selection.
f) Each option considered in a vacuum and not in comparison or contrast with the others.

Remember the importance involved in the words chosen in structuring the questions.

Poor wording can prevent you from getting the correct information instead of assisting you. Avoid moving your body or hands in a way that distracts the client instead of allowing them to go inside. Quiet observation is far more productive than talking to the subject too much.

Phrase your questions well, and then be silent so they can "go inside" to do the Transderivational Search necessary to come up with the information.

As you ask people to "Think of a time when...?" and you ask the various questions about their sequencing, the accessing cues become your clues as to sequencing of their strategy.

The eye movements and predicates provide particularly helpful tools.

These "beamers" will tell you the order in which the representation systems happen.

For instance, in a three part V-A-K strategy, you should be able to see (usually), three distinct eye movements.

Cycling through the strategy may take some time for some people and only a second or two for others. Eliciting strategies takes a lot of practice. However, it becomes easier after you have been doing it for a while.

Pointers in Elicitation

1. Use all the cues you get during elicitation.
2. Use repetition, that is, check them out.
3. Notice the non-verbal cues, specifically eye patterns and gestures.
4. Go for information in all rep systems.
5. Pay attention to the non-verbal information, such as marking out, tonality, etc.
6. Be sure to watch and listen for a strategy rather than installing one.
7. Use-counter examples (i.e. say something that you know they will disagree with, and check if they disagree) to help avoid installing anything.
8. Check for logical sequence.
9. Pay close attention: Does the person answer the question you ask?
Keep asking it until you get the answer.
10. Write down what you get only after you are sure you have it.
11. How much detailed (content) information you obtain has little importance. You want to gather process/structure information.
12. Seek contrast, i.e. "Did you do anything else?"

NLP allows us to "state control." And success at reaching desired outcomes (goals) comes to those who know how to manage state control, does it not?

And does not this, in fact, describe the difference between those who achieve their outcomes and those who fail to achieve their outcomes?

The difference lies in the ability to put yourself into supportive and enhancing states so that you can then produce the behaviours that move you to reach your goals.

The Skill of Elicitation

One of the most crucial NLP skills consists of the ability to do effective elicitation.

This skill enables you to discover the structure of subjective experiences wherever you find them in yourself and others.

The skill of eliciting also enables you to learn how to effectively transform experiences.

It plays a crucial role for effective communicating, persuading, motivating, etc.

1. Move to an up time state. Get all of your sense receptors open to inputting sights, sounds, sensations, etc.
2. Assist the person in accessing the state. This becomes important in order to elicit good clean information about a person's experience.

The person needs to get into the state. "Think about a time when you were honestly and completely confident (honest, forthright, in love, etc.)."

Eliciting the structure of almost any experience without that person being in state reduces your ability to explore effectively the state they are experiencing.
That removes it one level from the thing itself and will give you more of the person's theory about it rather than the experience itself.

3. Elicit as pure a state, or experience, as possible. If you ask for a "strong belief," pick something that the person doesn't have laden with emotionally significant issues, like, "I'm a worthwhile person."

Pick, "I believe the sun will rise tomorrow." "I believe in the importance of breathing."

The mental processes involve the same kind of thing, but the less emotionally laden content will give you "cleaner" information.

4. Express yourself congruently and evocatively.

In eliciting, remember that your tools consist of your words, your tones and your tempo, your physiology and other non-verbal signals. So be evocative, and sound like what you speak about.

5. Allow people time to process things.

If they aren't accessing, then have them pretend
(use the Pretend or "As if" frame): "What would it be
like if you could?"

6. Begin with unspecific words and unspecified
predicates (e.g. think, know, understand,
remember, experience, etc.).

This allows the person to search for the experience
in their own way.

7. Follow up with specific predicates.

As you notice the accessing of a certain rep system,
help them by then using sensory-specific words.
"And what do you see...?"

8. Use good downtime questions to assist the
person in locating and identifying the experience.

To do that you will need enough content so as to
ask good questions.

Downtime questions involve those questions the
answers to which are not on the edge of
consciousness.

The person has to go inside to their unconscious
mind to find the information.

9. Once the person begins accessing, focus on the form and structure of the experience by getting the person's submodality coding.

If the person gets stuck in trying to think of something, ask, "Do you know anyone who can?" "What would it be like if you stepped into their shoes for a few minutes and did it?"

Eliciting helps the person you're talking with to become conscious of factors normally outside their range of conscious awareness.

This means your own patience, positive expectation, and acceptance will make it easier (and safer) for the other person to access the information.

The desired outcome of NLP as a whole involves making accessible more resourcefulness in people.

To do that we need to have a general pattern for understanding how we get into "states" of mind-and-body, and how we can evaluate those states for resourcefulness.

APPENDIX

Visual Submodality Distinctions

Associated/Dissociated Framed (Shape, size, colour of Frame, etc.), Panoramic, Colour/Black & White, Colour Intensity/ Hue, Saturation (Vividness), Bright/Dim, Size of Picture, Central Objects, Fore/Background, Distance of Picture (Near/Far), Location in Space, Distance of Object from Self, 3-D or Flat, Contrast, Split Screen/Multiple Images Still or Movie, Movement (Fast/Slow), Direction Focus (Sharp/Fuzzy), Angle Viewed From, Steady Focus or Intermittent, Number of Pictures. Horizontal/Vertical, Sparkle, Point of View Angle of Image, Aspect Ratio (Height/Width) Tilt, Spin, etc. Digital (Words), Density (Graininess or 'Pixels'), Transparent/Opaque

Auditory Submodality Distinctions

Associated/Dissociated, Number of Sounds, Sources, Distance from You, Location in Space, Volume (Loud/Soft), Duration, Music/Noise/Voice, Contrast, Fore/Background, Tonality, Cadence, Timbre, Rhythm (Regular or Irregular), Clarity, Direction (Towards you or away from you)

Kinesthetic Submodality Distinctions

Pressure Still/Moving (where), Temperature,
Area/Extent Texture Vibration,
Intensity Moisture Number, Rhythm
Steady/Intermittent Size, Shape Weight
Internal/External, Duration Smell/Taste Other
Olfactory Submodality Distinctions
Organic (e.g. Roses) Inorganic (e.g. Sulphur) Other
Gustatory Submodality Distinctions
Bitter Sweet Sour Salty Other

Submodality Distinctions Common to All Systems

Associated/Disassociated Movement/Speed
Proximity (Distance), Intensity
Duration Direction, Spatial Location
Internal/External Frequency

Visual Predicates:

appear, bright, clear, colour, conspicuous, focus, hindsight, foresee, glance, image, vision, disappear, blind, illustrate, blurred, appear, vague, cloudy, enlighten, watch, observe, conceal, dark, dawn, display, farsighted, envision, overview, expose, form, foggy flash, features, peer, unsightly, graphic, perspective, picture, obscure, disappear, imagines, perspective, glance, glare, twinkle, vanish, glow, view, watch, visualize, gleam, show, veil, see, shiny, sight.....

Auditory Predicates:

Audible, babble, buzz, discord, earshot,
murmuring, drumming, droning, echo, listen, hiss,
loud, quiet, prattle, harmony, loud, muffled, noisy,
sound, squeal, answer, whisper, argue, announce,
rumble, roar, screech, attune, call, discuss,
grumble, crescendo, expression, chatter, complain,
sounds, gurgle, deaf, hear, explain, resonate,
Tune-in, hum, utter, lecture, shriek, melodious,
vocal, inquire, insult, silences, listen, outspoken,
hear, overtones, mention...

Kinaesthetic Predicates:

Bounce, fumble, soft, brush, tension, force, grope,
caress, carry, lukewarm, Sensuous, feel, poke,
plush, grinds, hustle, burdened, hold, clumsy, hug,
firm, tender, beat, kiss, impressed, grasp, pressure,
move, comfortable, strike, firm, crumble, pinch,
bends, flop, feel, exciting, angle, irritate, nudge,
shaky, rub, hard, break, hard, sensitive, mushy,
solid, pull.....

Olfactory/Gustatory Predicates:

Fragrant, taste, odour, pungent, smell, spicy, sour,
savour, fresh, smoky, salty, stale, bitter, sweet...

Unspecified Predicates:

Cognizant, conscious, conceive, clear, experience, decide, know, aware, believe, change, learn, process, question, sense, think, understand, motivate, nice, perceive, ponder, interest....

Sample Predicate Phrases

In the following order - Visual Auditory Kinesthetic (VAK)

- ✓ I see what you mean.

- ✓ I hear you loud and clear

- ✓ I get the point

- ✓ That brightens up my day.

- ✓ That rings a bell

- ✓ I have a gut feeling

- ✓ Just give me the big picture.

- ✓ It sounds like a plan

- ✓ I can't grasp it

- ✓ That's not clear to me.

- We are in tune with each other

- They rub me up the wrong way

- Point out what you mean.

- Don't hum and haw

- It hit me like a ton of bricks

- I was seeing red.

- It was music to my ears

- Moment of panic

- Get a new perspective

- In a manner of speaking

- Keep your shirt on

- It appears to me

- Word for word

- Hold fast/Hold on

- I have a mental picture

- Hold your tongue

- ✓ We need to get to grips with

- ✓ Looks like ...

- ✓ Voice an opinion

- ✓ Cool, calm & collected

- ✓ Right under your nose

- ✓ I'm all ears

- ✓ Chip off the old block

Favoured Representational Systems

V: Visual

People who are visual often stand or sit with their heads and/or bodies erect, with their eyes up. They usually breathe from the top of their lungs.

They memorize by seeing pictures, and are less distracted by noise. They often have trouble remembering verbal instructions because their minds tend to wander.

A visual person will be interested in how your idea looks. Appearances are important to them.

A: Auditory

People who are auditory will quite often move their eyes sideways.

They tend to breathe from the middle of their chest. They typically talk to themselves, and can be easily distracted by noise (Some even move their lips when they talk to themselves)

They can repeat things back to you easily, they learn by listening, and usually like music and talking on the phone. They memorize by steps, procedures, and sequences (sequentially). The auditory person likes to be TOLD how they're doing, and responds to a certain tone of voice or set of words. They will be interested in what you have to say about your idea.

K: Kinesthetic

People who are kinesthetic will typically be breathing from the bottom of their lungs, so you'll see their stomach go in and out when they breathe.

They often move and talk at a much slower rate than audio or visual people. They respond to physical rewards, and touching. They memorize by doing or walking through something. They will be interested in your idea if they can grasp it, or have a feel for it.

Ad: Auditory Digital

This person will spend a fair amount of time talking to themselves.

They will want to know if your idea "makes sense". The auditory digital person can exhibit characteristics of the other major representational systems.

Elicitation Questions for Eye Accessing Patterns

Visual Remembered (Vr): Seeing images from memory, recalling things they have seen before.

Question: "What is the colour of your front door?"

Visual Constructed (Vc): Images of things that people have never seen before. When people are making it up in their head, they are using visual constructed.

Question: "What would your bedroom look like if it were pink check with orange dots?"

Auditory Remembered (Ar): When you remember sounds or voices that you've heard before, or things that you've said to yourself before.

QUESTION: "What was the very last thing I said?"

Auditory Constructed (Ac): Making up sounds you have not heard before.

Question: "What would I sound like if I had Mickey Mouse's voice?"

Auditory Digital (Ad): This is where your eyes go when you are talking to yourself — internal dialogue.

234

Question: "Can you save the Lord's Prayer to yourself?"

Kinesthetic (K): (Feelings, sense of touch.) Generally you look in this direction when you are accessing your feelings.

Question: "What does it feel like to walk on the grass in bare feet?"

Some people access Vr, Ar, Ad or K by defocusing. Watch closely and remember once you have their cues they usually remain the same.

Stacking Anchors

Purpose: To amplify a resource state.
We stack anchors by anchoring several similar
states on the same place.

1. Identify a positive resourceful state. Elicit the
state and associate. Anchor it. Release the anchor.

2. Break state

3. Elicit several more positive states separately and
anchor each one in the same spot as the first
anchor. Use as many states as you need to in order
to achieve an extremely powerful state.

4. Test anchor.

Collapse Anchor

Purpose: To add a resource to a negative state. To release negative feelings.

This process has a definite purpose and involves establishing a positive anchor sufficient in collapsing or overcoming the negative anchor.

On a scale from one to ten, have your client rate the strength of the negative state.

A negative anchor will be at the higher end of the scale, usually a 10.

With each positive state, have them rate them in relation to the strength of the original negative state.

As you stack the positive states in whatever unique anchor you have selected the client then gives you a new/current rating for the negative state.

You keep on adding these positive states until the total exceeded ten. Once the positive anchor has

become stronger than the negative, fire both anchors simultaneously.
Your client may well enter a state of confusion.

Release the negative anchor first, leave a slight delay and then release the positive anchor.

The procedure is very powerful.

Your client likely will recall the experience but the negativity associated with it will either be gone entirely or greatly diminished.

The process is below step by step for this very effective therapeutic technique.

1. Identify a positive resourceful state.
2. Identify a negative state.
3. Elicit the positive state and associate fully into the state. Just before the state begins to peak (calibrate), and set anchor. Break state. Test Anchor.
4. Elicit the negative state. Associate fully. Set Anchor. Break State. Test Anchor.
5. Fire off both anchors (Positive & Negative) at the same time. Hold anchors until they peak. (Subject will often have a "puzzled" look on their face.)
6. Release negative anchor first. Hold the positive anchor (All) for 5 seconds and then release.
7. Test. Fire the negative anchor and calibrate how the experience has changed.

NLP Presuppositions

1. "The map is not the territory"

2. "People respond according to their internal maps"

3. "Meaning operates context-dependently"

4. "Mind-and-body inevitably and inescapably affects each other"

5. "Individual skills function by developing and sequencing of our representational systems"

6. "We respect each person's model of the world"

7. "Person and behaviour are different phenomena. We are not our behaviour"

8. "Every behaviour has usefulness—all behaviour comes from positive intensions"

9. "We evaluate behaviour & change in terms of context and ecology"

10. "We cannot not communicate"

11. "The way we communicate affects perception & reception"

12. "The meaning of communication lies in the response you get"

13. "The one who sets the frame for the communication controls the action"

14. "There is no failure, only feedback'

15. "The person with the most flexibility exercises the most influence in the system"

16. "Resistance indicates the lack of rapport"

17. "People have the internal resources they need to succeed"

18. "Humans have the ability to experience one-trial learning"

19. "All communication should increase choice"

20. "People make the best choices open to them when they act"

21. "As response-able persons, we can run our own brain and control our results"

Meta Model

Nominalizations: Linguistically, nominalization refers to changing a Deep Structure process (movement, action, etc.) into a Surface Structure static event.

Mind Reading: We engage in mind reading when we think and assert that we know the thoughts, motives, intentions, etc., in another's mind.

Cause-Effect: The over-used accusation, "You make me mad!" illustrates a cause-effect statement.

Complex Equivalence: We generate a complex equivalence whenever we use a part of an experience (an aspect of the external behaviour) to become equivalent to the whole of its meaning (our internal state).

Presuppositions: By the term presupposition, we refer to the conceptual and linguistic assumptions that have to exist in order for a statement to make sense.

Universal Quantifiers: A universal quantifier refers to the set of words that make a universal generalization.

Modal Operators: This linguistic distinction refers to our mode whereby we operate in the world.

Lost Performative: When we perform upon our world with value judgments, we speak about important values that we believe in.

Comparative Deletions: In a comparative deletion someone makes a comparison, but deletes either the specific persons, things, or items compared or the standard by which the speaker makes the comparison.

Unspecified Verb: Unspecified verbs describe vague, non-specific action.

Submodalities Worksheet

Milton Model Hypnotic Language Patterns

1. Mind Read: Claiming to know the thoughts or
feelings of another without specifying the process
by which you came to know the info.
"I know that you are wondering..."

2. Lost Performative: Value judgments (which may include an unspecified comparison) where the performer of the value judgment is left out.
"And it's a good thing to wonder..."

3. Cause & Effect: Where it is implied that one thing causes another (Including attribution of cause outside of self.)

4. Complex Equivalence: Where two things are equated – as in their meanings being equivalent.
"That means..."

5. Presupposition: The linguistic equivalent of assumptions.

"You are learning many things..."

6. Universal Quantifier: A set of words which has:
   a. A universal generalization and
   b. No referential index.

"And all the things, all the things..."

7. Modal Operator: Words, which implies possibility or necessity, which often form our rules in life.

"That you can learn..."

8. Nominalization: Process words (including verbs), which have been frozen in time by making them into nouns.

"Provide you with new insights, and new understandings."

9. Unspecified Verb: Where an adjective or adverb modifier does not specify the verb.

"And you can,"

10. Tag Question: A question added after a statement, designed to displace resistance.

11. Lack of Referential Index: A phrase, which does not pick out a specific portion of the listener's experience.

"One can, you know..."
12. Comparative Deletion: Where the comparison is made and it is not specified as to what or whom it was made.

"And it's more or less the right thing."

13. Pace Current Experience: Where client's verifiable, external experience is described in a way, which is undeniable.

"You are sitting here, listening to me, looking at me, (etc.)..."

14. Double Bind: Where the client is given two choices (both of which are preferable or desired) separated by an "or".

"And that means that your unconscious mind is also here, and can hear (phonological ambiguity) what I say. And since that's the case, you are probably learning about this and already know more at an unconscious level than you think you do.
So, it's not right for me to tell you, learn this or learn that, learn in any way you want, in any order."

15. Conversational Postulate: The communication has the form of a question – a question to which the response is either a 'yes' or a 'no'.

If I want you to do something, what else must be present so that you will do it, and out of your awareness?

It allows you to choose to respond or not and avoids authoritarianism.

"Do you feel this...? (Punctuation ambiguity) is something you understand?"

16. Extended Quotes: Quotes which are extended beyond what is normally used to displace resistance.

"Last week I was with Richard who told me about his training in 1983 at Denver when he talked to someone who said..."

17. Selectional Restriction Violation: A sentence that is not well formed in that only humans and animals can have feelings.

"A chair can have feelings..."

"Remember, the walls have ears."

18. Ambiguity:

a. Phonological: Where two words with different meanings sound the same.

   i.e.: "Hear", "Here"

b. Syntactic: Where the function (syntactic) of a word cannot be immediately determined from the immediate context.

   "They are visiting relatives"
"Selling salesmen can be tricky!"
   "I am really over managing managers."
c. Scope: Where it cannot be determined by linguistic context how much is applied to that sentence by some other portion of the sentence.

   "Speaking to you as a child..."

"The old men & women..."
"The disturbing noises & thoughts..."
"The weight of your hands & feet..."

    d. Punctuation: Either the punctuation is eliminated as in a run on sentence or pauses occur in the wrong place.

"I want you to notice your hand me the glass."

19. Utilization: Remember to utilize all that happens or is said.

Client says: "I am not sold."
Response: "That's right you are not sold, yet, because you haven't asked the one question that will have you totally and completely sold."

Putting it all together

"I know that you are wondering... and it's a good thing to wonder... because... that means... you are learning many things... and all the things, all the things... that you can learn... provide you with new insights, and new understandings. And you can, can you not? One can, you know. And it's more or less the right thing. You are sitting here, listening to me, looking at me, and that means that your unconscious mind is also here, and can hear what I say. And since that's the case, you are probably learning about this and already know more at an unconscious level than you think you do, and it's

not right for me to tell him, learn this or learn that,
let him learn in any way he wants, in any order. Do
you feel this... is something you understand?
Because, last week I was with Milton who told me
about his training in 1979 in Miami when he talked
to someone who said, "A chair can have feelings..."

NLP Terminology

Accessing Cues
Shifts in breathing, posture, gestures and eye
    movements that indicate internal mental
    processing such as visualisation, auditory and
    kinaesthetic activity.

Accreditation
Having official recognition by a national
    government through a government body,
    government department, Act of Parliament or
    Royal Charter with reference to a set of
    government approved standards. In the case of
    educational or vocational courses,
    accreditation confers recognition of the
    qualification offered and an assurance of
    adherence to a government approved set of
    standards for quality.

Aligned Perceptual Positions
A term coined by Connirae Andreas to describe the
    process she developed to achieve clearly well
    sorted perceptual positions. When in First
    Position, seeing out of your own eyes, hearing
    with your ears at their location, and feeling in
    your own body, with only your feelings. When
    in Third Position, seeing self and other,
    hearing both of them, and only experiencing
    feelings about the interaction. When in Second

Position, seeing, hearing and feeling as if the other. See perceptual positions. Each perceptual position has a particular organisation as a means of accessing high quality information.

Analogue
Continuous change over time: continuous movement. An example is the light dimmer switch in contrast to an ordinary light switch which is either on or off (digital).

Analogue Shaping
Shaping the body posture, breathing and movements of the subject.

Anchoring
Applying a gesture, touch, or sound just before a state peaks, either in oneself or someone else, so that the *anchored* state can be re-activated by reapplying that gesture, touch or sound. A smell can also be used as an anchor. Eg. As you remember the smell of a rose, you may find a memory of some experience that involved roses coming to mind. Psychologists recognise the pattern of anchoring as stimulus response conditioning.

Anthropology
The study of man in his / her various environments.

As If frame

A way of shifting into a different perceptual
framework, and thus obtaining another quality
of information. This can be especially useful if
the content you are thinking about involves a
stuck feeling. To use an "as if" frame, think of
what it would be like *As if* you had the needed
resource.

Associated

Experiencing the present with all your attention;
seeing, hearing and feeling the living action
that is taking place in the moment. For
referring to memory or imagination, living a
past or future experience from your viewpoint
of the time; seeing, hearing and feeling as if
you are present in that moment.

Attention

The use of external senses and internal
representational systems to identify and
choose the content of thoughts and activities.
Attention can be conscious or unconscious or
a combination of both. Where one places one's
conscious or unconscious attention has an
effect on cognitive processes. First attention or
the attention of the conscious mind is limited.
(See conscious awareness). Second attention
refers to the processes and organisation of the
unconscious mind.

Auditory Processing

The processing of sounds, this could be in the form of language, music or noise. Includes the ability to have internal dialogue, recalled information such as remembering someone's voice, recall of music or the construction of words, or composition of music.

Backtrack
A review, both verbal and non-verbal, of the last portion of a discussion, presentation or set of instructions.

Behaviour
Any human activity, this includes internal thought processes, such as visual, auditory or kinaesthetic processing and involuntary as well as involuntary movement such as blinking or heart beat.

Behavioural Psychology
A school of psychology which deletes internal cognitive processes from its descriptions of psychology. An example of Western society's predilection for first attention.

Behavioural Technologies
Systems and models of psychology orientated to changing and extending human behaviour.

Beliefs

Subjective ideas about what is true and not true for
    ourselves and the world, developed through
    exposure to experience, and modified by
    perceptual filters of distortion, generalisation
    and deletion. A configuration of Submodalities
    that lets a person who holds content in those
    Submodalities know that content is true for
    them.

Calibration
Learning to recognise visible, auditory and
    kinaesthetic clues to an individual's use of
    their mental processes. Defining that
    individual's expressions by comparing their
    present behaviour with their previously
    observed behaviour.

Capability
A context specific skill that can be broken down to
    its component behaviours.

Chain of Excellence
An essential element of the New Code of NLP
    developed by John Grinder. The Chain of
    Excellence has four stages.
Breathing - a leverage point for change. It affects
Physiology - change physiology and shift
State - change state and affect - Performance.

Choice Points

Moments of subjective experience which generate
significant consequences thereafter.

Chunking
Grouping information by class and subclass,
especially useful when combined with the
principles of logical typing order. Chunking
develops meaning and thereby facilitates
memory. (See logical levels).

Cognitive/analytical modelling
The conscious elicitation of the components of the
skills of an expert. May include verbal
descriptions of beliefs, values, outcomes,
intentions, sequences and processes used by
the expert. This form of modelling is outside
the scope of NLP as it is of a different logical
type from the patterns of excellence that make
up the field. Analytical modelling depends on
conscious recognition of elements of expertise
by the expert and the person modelling and on
conscious uptake by the modeller. See NLP
Modelling.

Cognitive Psychology
Cognition is defined by Strobe, Codol and
Stephenson in their book *Introducing Social
Psychology* as "The activity by which
information is received, selected, transformed
and organised by human perceivers so as to
construct representations of reality and to
build knowledge".

Cognitive Science
A multi-disciplinary field of inquiry into the
perceptions of the mind. Cognitive science
draws on methodology and learning from
linguistics, psychology, philosophy, artificial
intelligence and computer science.

Complex Equivalent
The individual's *cognitive map* or sensory
representation of a particular word, label or
expression; the meaning they assign to an
abstract form of words. A different experience
or action that has the same meaning for an
individual as the experience they are
considering. Misunderstanding occurs when
two individuals each assign meaning to an
abstract word or phrase and then act as if they
were using a shared, defined meaning.

Congruence
The match of a person's body language (gestures,
posture and voice patterns) with their verbal
output (auditory digital) while they are
communicating. Congruence in
communication is one of the patterns found in
charismatic people. Note though, when a
person is communicating with congruency,
this is not necessarily an indicator of truth,
rationality or sensibility in terms of the
content communicated. It means that in the
moment, they believe what they are saying. Eg.

Hitler communicated congruently, yet many of his ideas (content), were unecological in their effect on third parties.

Conscious awareness
The conscious mind is limited in terms of the amount of information that can be held at any one moment in time to seven plus or minus two chunks. The size of the chunks is variable. A metaphoric description is the experience of shining a torch around a darkened room. As the light beam moves from one place to another, you notice different items. You can never see the entire contents of the room with the torch light. Like the torch, conscious attention shifts from one experience to another.

Content Reframing
Can be of two forms; either changing the response to an experience by changing the meaning of the experience in that context, (meaning reframe), or leaving the meaning of the behaviour the same and placing the behaviour in a different context (context reframing).

Context
The situation, time and place within which designated activity takes place.

Criterion (S), Criteria (P)

An individual's or organisation's definition of what
is important to them in terms of their
particular standards and values.

Cross-pacing
Taking any repetitive behaviour on the part of the
subject, and matching that behaviour through
a different communication channel. You could
speak in time to the subject's breathing. If the
person is blinking, you could tap a pencil in
time to their blink rate. Cross-pacing builds
rapport with the person's unconscious mind
and is a subtle, less noticeable approach to
building or maintaining rapport than
mirroring the subject's behaviour directly.

Cultural conditioning
The assimilation of beliefs, values and ways of one's
culture of upbringing is sometimes referred to
as cultural conditioning. We have all been
shaped to a greater or lesser extent by the
social context in which we grew-up, and by the
social, political, economic and cultural
contexts in which we live subsequently. One of
the benefits of the models Neuro-Linguistic
Programming and Ericksonian hypnosis is the
capability to evaluate the various belief
systems that one adopted, and to update,
change and enrich those *maps* of reality if so
desired. This process brings added flexibility
and choice into one's life.

Culture
The generally agreed upon maps within a
    particular community of people which guide
    behaviour. These agreed upon maps form
    collectively a consensus reality for the group
    and generally operate outside conscious
    awareness.

Cybernetic epistemology (systems epistemology)
An orientation to pattern and the relationship
    between parts of a system, rather than using
    quantification, and reductionism as in
    Newtonian physics. Cybernetic epistemology is
    based on the premise that living systems such
    as a person, family or ecology functions on
    different rules to the world of physics. (See
    Epistemology and Systems Thinking).

Cybernetics
The study of communication systems in both man
    and machines. Cybernetics has been
    traditionally applied to machines, computer
    systems and computer software. Cybernetics
    can also be applied to the individual, the
    family (as in the family systems models) and
    social systems such as communities and
    societies.

Deep Trance Identification
A hypnotic process where the subject enters a
    profoundly altered state and makes

arrangements through his or her unconscious
mind, in trance, to model specific or general
patterns displayed by the model of excellence.

Deletion
The process of excluding portions of experience of
the world from one's internal representations,
and one's speech.

Description (map, model)
An internal representation that we have that guides
our behaviour. Primarily we have sensory
representational systems, that is, we represent
the world in mental images, soundtracks and
sensation. There is also secondary
representation, language. i.e. we can represent
our internal pictures, sounds and feelings in
language.

Digital
Sudden change in state. A standard light switch is
digital, it can only be on or off.

Discovery Frame
Involves a psychological state, (see *State*) and an
attitude in terms of perception. Expectation,
judgement and desire are suspended for the
duration of the exercise in order to discover
what happens to one's perceptions and ideas
as a result of participating in it. That subjective
state and attitude in relation to the wider

world. i.e. the expert being modelled and / or
the world at large.

Dissociation
The process of stepping outside the point of view
of experiencing the world from one's physical
position; seeing oneself from outside the self
and, for internal representations, from outside
the image and separate from the sounds.

Distortion
Inaccurate reproduction of events in any recording
medium, including human representation.
Distortion in language refers to demonstrably
inaccurate comments on any subject.

Dovetailing Outcomes
Two or more parties' outcomes, in which the
achievement of one facilitates achievement of
the other(s). The first step in negotiating
anything is to elicit all parties' outcomes, then
derive a common set of outcomes by chunking
up to a higher logical level. At this point the
outcomes are said to be dovetailed.

Down time
The process of putting one's attention to internal
processes and representations within one's
mind.

Ecology

The process of considering the effects of any
change in behaviour across a number of time
frames, situations and places for self and
others. What are the consequences now, in the
future, for oneself, for significant others, in
various contexts such as home, career,
lifestyle, as well as possible effects on the
physical environment. The use of the answers
to these questions is determined by the values
held important by that individual.

Elegance
In NLP elegance describes the performance of a
particular pattern in a streamlined, efficient,
and natural way. Elegance denotes the
minimum activity that is necessary and
sufficient to produce the desired outcome with
acceptable and ecological consequences. "The
minimal number of distinctions necessary to
provide an effective replication of the talent"
(Grinder, DeLozier and Bandler, 1977).

Elicitation
The art through communication of getting a
particular response or piece of information
from someone. As practitioners of
Neuro-Linguistic Programming and
Ericksonian hypnosis, we are involved in
eliciting from clients the resources they need
to take themselves from the present state to
their desired outcome.

Emotion

A sequence of internal representations and
   external sensory input, usually ending with a
   kinaesthetic (hence the colloquial term
   "feeling"). An emotion may occur in response
   to sensory input or internal representation,
   whether these activities are conscious or
   unconscious. Compare with "Thought; a
   sequence of internal representations and
   external sensory input".

Emotional states - mapping and shifting

It is possible to unpack and define the structure of
   emotional states, whether experienced as
   enhancing or limiting to the individual. Once a
   particular emotion has been mapped out, the
   structure of the state in question can be
   altered if desired, to create something more
   useful for oneself.

Endorsement

A statement of recognition or approval from a
   non-official and non-government body or
   individual. Can be a signal honour and provide
   a boost to credibility when given by a credible
   or knowledgeable person. Endorsement does
   not denote or confer official recognition nor
   accreditation.

Epistemology

The study of how we know what we know, how
   creatures or groups of creatures, including

humans, from families to cultures, societies and the global living system, think, and decide. It reveals the premises underlying outer behaviour and inner thinking. These premises may be based on the history of society and the individual, and they set filters which allow or limit the passage of new information of difference into the mind. Sub-systems such as an individual or a family may have a particular epistemology. Systems such as an extended family, culture or society may have a dominant epistemology, and the greater system of interconnected life has a number of epistemologies. The dominant epistemology of the West is still based on Cartesian mind-body dualism, although some thinkers perceive this to be in error. They believe it to be a major contribution to the present imbalance and damage to the greater system of life on earth.

Ericksonian Hypnosis
Communication models developed from studies of the innovative psychiatrist Dr Milton H. Erickson, for working with an individual's subjective experience. In contrast to traditional Hypnosis, which uses ritual inductions and direct suggestion, Ericksonian hypnosis stresses the importance of respecting the uniqueness of each individual and the development of trance states shaped for that person. Subsequently, an Ericksonian approach to hypnosis involves calibration, the

use of context and indirect suggestion to
    facilitate learning within the individual. In
    Ericksonian hypnosis the relationship between
    guide and subject is important, and therefore
    attention is given to rapport, communication,
    high quality information gathering and
    feedback.

Ethnology
The comparative study of the behaviour of
    creatures, which include humans, living in
    their natural environment. Used to be known
    as 'natural history' before humans were
    included in the study.

Eye Accessing Cues
The directional movements of the eyes which
    indicate the accessing of different modes of
    thinking, or representational systems. These
    are visual recall and construction, auditory
    recall and construction, kinaesthetic (feeling,
    proprioception, sensation), and internal
    dialogue or auditory digital.

Features
A chosen distinction that one attends to while
    observing the model expressing the target
    capability. Some of the features Neuro
    Linguistic Programmers traditionally attend to
    are eye accessing cues, changes in skin colour,
    muscle tone, voice tonality, and voice rhythm.

Through careful observation one may detect a
new feature that operates in some sort of
pattern. Within the NLP community the term
distinctions is used interchangeably with
features.

Feedback
The set of mechanisms that let you know whether
or not you are moving towards your desired
outcome.

Feldenkrais method
A system of movement re-education developed by
the nuclear physicist Moshe Feldenkrais. The
Feldenkrais method works with the patterns of
movement, breathing and posture and
re-imprints new, more functional patterns
into the nervous system. The Feldenkrais
technology has been referred to as the NLP of
the body because of its 'systemic thinking'
approach. See systemic thinking.

First Order Change
Change occurring on the same logical level as the
problem state. Eg acting on behaviour to
obtain a change in behaviour.

First Position
The act of looking out of one's own eyes, hearing
with one's ears, feeling, tasting and scenting,
using one's own organs within one's body, and
making one's own internal representations.

Flexibility

An extended range of behavioural responses that
can be drawn upon. Each sensory channel has
an extended range of ways of recalling and
constructing representations. Also an
extended range of emotional responses which
can be elicited, created and expressed for each
situation encountered by the individual. At a
more complex level of processing, flexibility
describes access to an extended range of
perceptual filters. The use of flexibility is in its
application to any given context, such that the
individual can use behaviour which serves
them in that context, whether conventionally
accepted or otherwise, with reference to their
own ecology.

Frame

The context surrounding a given set of events and
behaviour, imparting meaning to those
interactions by its presence.

Future Pace

The process of placing new or desired behaviours,
capabilities and or perceptual filters into the
future for use in appropriate times and places.
(See *Simulation Programming*).

Generalisation

The act of taking a specific incident or behaviour and generalising the content across contexts, as if it were a generic pattern. Eg "people always do that", or "if it works at all, it will work everywhere".

Generative Change
A change that creates the possibility of further change ensuing through time as a result of the initial change taking place. Eg. Feeding someone for a day provides three free meals only. Teaching them to fish enables them to provide their own food, earn their living, and teach others. That is a generative change.

Genius State
An up-time resource state in which an individual's attention is directed outwards, into the environment. Often it includes long distance and peripheral vision, an absence of internal dialogue, and optimal physiological posture and movement. It often includes awareness of well formed outcomes, how to act *as if*, the ability to construct pictures and sounds, to use multiple perceptual positions, different logical levels, and conscious/unconscious interface.

Gestalt
The totality of an experience at all logical levels and in all senses.

Gestalt psychology

A school of psychology.

Gustatory
Pertaining to taste.

Homeostasis
Literally, the stillness of sameness. A state of
    stability.

Hypnosis
The art of altering another person's state, usually
    applied to deliberate trance induction and
    utilisation.

Identity
The conventional concepts of self image, self
    esteem and self concept are examples of
    identity. In this work the construct of identity
    includes the way we see, hear and feel about
    ourselves. An identity representation of this
    type, aligned and matching in all senses is a
    significant pattern found in individuals who
    are able to bring their dreams to fruition.

Imprint
In most animals imprinting is the triggering of an
    innate instinctive behaviour, such as
    attachment to parents or parent substitutes,
    during a critical or sensitive time period. With
    most animals imprinting is irreversible. In

humans imprinting is reversible, and takes
place in many formative situations in which
beliefs and values are learned.

Incongruence
A partial or divided response which is indicative of
    uncertainty in the mind of the respondent. An
    incongruent response can be elicited in
    someone by offering them incongruent
    communication (mixed messages) or
    insufficient information with which to operate.
    Where internal conflict is already apparent,
    there is a shortage of information in the
    individual's own system. Incongruence can be
    simultaneous, as described, or sequential, in
    which case the subject appears to be
    congruent in favour of an action while in a
    given state and equally congruently against the
    same action when in a different state.

Information
Gregory Bateson describes information as *news of
    difference* (*Mind and Nature; A necessary unity*,
    1979). Our sensory apparatus and neurology
    responds to difference in the world as
    information.

Integration
Integration is the act of embodying learned
    material, and is mediated through the
    vestibular apparatus. This specialised sense
    enables us to live in the whole of ourselves;

experience states of pleasure and is involved
   with spatial orientation and movement
   towards our outcomes in the external world.

Intention
The reason or purpose behind a specific piece of
   behaviour. The answer to the question, "What
   did you do that for?". Intention is not always
   apparent from behaviour, and is deemed to be
   positive, at least for the person doing the
   behaviour, according to their model of the
   world.

Internal negotiation
The act of separating out different parts of oneself
   which appear to want different and conflicting
   outcomes for the whole person. Having
   elicited each part's outcome, one can ascertain
   the function of each outcome, and chunk up
   through logical levels to a point where each
   part shares beliefs, values and a common
   outcome. It is then possible to align the parts
   to the common cause, and sometimes
   integrate them into each other.

Internal representation
The pictures, sounds and feelings that we make on
   the inside; our thoughts. Our internal
   representations, also known as mental maps,
   govern our behaviour in the world.

In Time

A state in which the individual perceives the
passage of time as continuous in the present,
where the future has limited importance and
the past is no longer relevant.

Kinesics
The formal study of body language.

Kinaesthetic
Pertaining to feeling, touching, proprioception,
sensation.

Leading
Using verbal and non-verbal communication to
elicit a desired response from another person.
Usually proceeded by pacing, to establish
rapport prior to leading.

Lead System
The first sensory system to take in information
from the outside. Can be outside conscious
awareness. The lead system was once thought
to be relatively constant in an individual, but
according to Grinder (Boulder; Pattern
Detection 1996) the lead system is subject to
change. The lead system is the first element in
any strategy.

Linguistics

The formal study of languages. In English
linguistics is broken into the following major
areas of study; phonology, the study of
phonemes the basic components of sound in
spoken language, morphology, the smallest
meaningful components of words, syntax, the
rules or grammar of language and semantics,
the meaning of language. Syntax is an
important component of Neuro-Linguistic
Programming as the order and sequence of
utterances has a profound effect on the
meaning of what is said.

Logical Levels
A system for organising representations
(information) into classes and sub-classes. eg.
Apples are a member of the class fruit which
belongs to the class food. Food occupies a
higher logical level than apple. An example of
the same logical level as apple is pear, and a
specific (lower logical level) example of apple is
Sturmer. Logical levels are useful for
categorising and remembering information.
Given the concept of seven plus or minus two
chunks of information, one has a choice in this
example of holding in conscious attention
seven kinds of apples, seven kinds of fruit,
seven kinds of food etc, according to the chunk
size adopted.

Macro modelling

An example of cognitive modelling. Constructing a
model of the broader context (situation, time
and place) where the expert successfully
expresses the target capability, as well as using
content categories such as Dilts Neurological
levels. These activities all fall outside the scope
of NLP being of different logical types.

Micro modelling
Building descriptions of specific thought processes
used by a model within a specific context. A
series of micro models, making up a complex
capability. Another example of cognitive
modelling.

Map
In NLP map is a general term synonymous with
description or subjective representation of
reality.

Map of Reality
Reference to NLP presupposition, "The map is not
the territory". If everything a person senses is
at one remove from external reality, then their
representations constitute a map.

Meta–cognition
Thinking about one's thought processes from an
outside perspective (meta-position).

Meta Model

A Meta model is a model of a model. In the world of NLP the Meta Model refers to a language tool developed by John Grinder and Richard Bandler to enable users to verify, clarify and specify imprecise verbal and written communication. The Meta Model provides questions to elicit information which previously was distorted, generalised and deleted.

Meta modelling
The process of building Models for describing models. See Strategies.

Metaphor
A description of a set of circumstances designed to replicate the patterns of a *real* set of circumstances, used to offer solutions and suggestions or learning. Often used to allow learning to occur directly through the unconscious mind. Includes allegory and simile.

Meta Programs
Content descriptions of some of the ways in which people can and do place their attention. The first Meta programs were described by John Grinder as a humorous method of showing the distinction between patterns and content models for his students at UCSC. The distinction is made by chunking up from a content example to the pattern that informs it.

Meta programs were taken up by Leslie Cameron-Bandler and her colleagues and used for profiling people. Cameron-Bandler now identifies Meta programs as content. As a content model, Meta program categorisation and use has no place in the context of NLP.

Methodology
A set of tools, techniques, procedures and investigative methods, used to collect, store, analyse and present information. Scientific methodology involves the development of hypotheses and predictions, investigating the manipulation of particular variables while maintaining all other variables constant, using measurable, objective measures and statistical analyses in order to come to conclusions about the topic under investigation.

Milton Model
The Milton Model is a reflection of the Meta Model, in that it has the exact opposite function. It was developed by John Grinder, Richard Bandler, and Judith DeLozier after they modelled the psychiatrist and hypnotist Dr. Milton H. Erickson. Instead of filling in the gaps in language left by distortion generalisation and deletion, the Milton Model deliberately distorts, generalises and deletes information to offer direction for thought with non-specific content. This allows each listener to construct or remember their own

experience within the framework offered by the speaker or writer. Examples where the Milton Model is used include Hypnotic induction and utilisation, political speeches and religious ceremonial language.

Mismatching
Doing something differently from another person with the result that rapport is broken. For example, breathing at a different rate, speaking more quickly or slowly than the other. Can be conscious or unconscious.

Mission Statement
A general statement of a vision in word form. It is important to have a rich representation of the vision in all the senses. Then the mission statement can be written in language which allows all parties to it to derive meaning from it, yet be precise enough to guide them towards achieving it. It is a general statement of intent, normally restricted to five or six lines of type.

Modelling (modelling) see also, (replicating talent) (NLP Modelling)
The effective description, replication and transfer of human capabilities from one person to another. It includes the detection of patterns of behaviour, the relationship of those patterns to a particular context, and some intended outcome. When modelling, we elicit and

describe a series of templates of the thinking patterns used by an expert in the course of their expertise. We develop models within the framework of elegance, that is using the minimal number of distinctions necessary to provide an effective replication of the talent (Grinder, DeLozier & Bandler, 1977). By removing any inessential features the capability is streamlined. A form of learning where a person is exposed to the behaviours and qualities of a significant other, which leads to the representation, internalising and later expression of those behaviours and or qualities. Examples include children modelling parents, students modelling a mentor or teacher, and the apprenticeship system. When done deliberately, modelling is the elicitation and replication of particular skills and expertise from a chosen expert in that field. Often the most valuable components of their skills were previously outside their conscious awareness.

Modal Operator
Linguistic term referring to words which denote requirement or options. Cited in meta-model as modal operators of necessity (should, must, have to) and modal operators of possibility (might, could).

Model of the World

The sum total of an individual's beliefs and values, perceptual filters, desires and expectations, experiences and learning's about the world. Each person has a unique combination of the above. As human beings, our behaviour is governed by how we perceive, believe, and think about ourselves and the world. It is our internal representation of reality, and the processes we use to organise our internal representations that shape our actions. These internal *maps* and the relationships within our minds are referred to as our *model of the world*.

Multiple Descriptions
We act on and through our maps of reality rather than on the world directly. Having and using multiple maps of the world offer distinct advantages over any single map. Different descriptions for different circumstances, as well as multiple descriptions for a particular context add richness in terms of possible choices in how to act and be in the world. A minimum of three examples of any given skill, concept or activity, thus allowing the learner to cross refer and understand in depth. The purpose of creating multiple descriptions is to enable the individual to access a wider range of information, including that which may have been outside their awareness. That having and using multiple maps of the world offer distinct advantages over any single map. Different descriptions for different circumstances, as

well as multiple descriptions for a particular context add richness in terms of possible choices in how to act and be in the world.

Multiple Intelligences
In this model it is presupposed that individuals in Western society are exposed to many different experiences, and that it is norm for an individual to develop different capabilities and mental strategies, expressed as multiple intelligences. These are commonly listed as visual, spatial, linguistic, musical, physical, and numerical, and they cover a broader range of activity than that which is measured in IQ tests.

Neuro Linguistic Programming
NLP models patterns of human excellence. This includes the way people of excellence take in information from the world, how they describe it to themselves with their senses, filter it with their beliefs and values, and act on the result. In summary there is a person, their descriptions and the world; and NLP studies the relationships between them.
NLP Application is the application of NLP modelled patterns to topics and contexts where they can contribute. NLP Training is the art of enabling others to learn the patterns of NLP and to distinguish patterns from content. NLP Training using the New Code methodology is

the art of enabling others to learn the patterns
of NLP accurately and generatively through
discovery and unconscious uptake, before they
become conscious of what they are doing.

Neuro-logical Levels
A list of specific content categories, developed by
Robert Dilts to assist people to sort their ideas.
Refers to environment, behaviour, capability,
belief, identity, mission. Called "Neuro-logical"
levels because in Dilts' opinion, the further up
the list, the more neurology is involved in the
experience. Does not belong in the field of NLP
being of a different logical type.

Neuroscience
A branch of psychology, also called physiological
psychology. Neuroscience is the study of the
functioning of the nervous system which
includes the structures and functioning of the
brain and its relationship to behaviour.

New Code
A description of NLP which uses a systemic
approach to demonstrate and teach the
patterns by providing a series of contexts in
which they manifest spontaneously. In the
New Code of NLP the unconscious of the client
is explicitly assigned the responsibility for the
selection of the critical elements-the desired
state, the resource, or new behaviour. The
unconscious is explicitly involved in all steps.

There are precise constraints placed upon the selection of new behaviour, more specifically, the new behaviour must satisfy the original positive intention(s) of the behaviour to be changed. The manipulation occurs at the level of state and intention as opposed to that of behaviour. (Grinder, Bostic 2000).

NLP Modelling
A five step process described by Grinder and Bostic in "Whispering in the Wind" (2000). This is the form of modelling which is taught in NLP.
Identify one or more appropriate models of excellence in the skill to be modelled.
Model implicitly by unconscious uptake for as long as it takes, with explicit intent to refuse to allow conscious analysis, understanding or coding.
Continue implicit modelling until as competent as the model and performing at that level of competence and in the same time frame as the model. Continue to use the skill unconsciously. For practical purposes this is the last step in the process.
If there is a need to make the skill explicit, only do it after a period of practice with the skill after modelling is complete. Allow the patterns to become conscious and choose an appropriate form of coding for the explication of the model.

Teach the patterns you have identified and coded
to someone else. The evidence of your
accuracy will be in their behaviour.

Nominalization
A verb which has been turned into an abstract
noun. Ie the name of something which cannot
be put in a wheelbarrow, or described as an
'Ongoing X'. Eg decision, revision, opposition.

Olfactory
Pertaining to the sense of smell.

Other than conscious Mind
Another way of describing the unconscious mind.
That which is outside conscious awareness.

Outcomes
In Neuro-Linguistic Programming a representation
of what we want in a specific context, involving
all representational systems. To be
well-formed, an outcome is also stated in
positive terms, has defined resources that the
individual can get access to, is within the
individual's control, has demonstrable
evidence and is ecological.

Overlap
A language pattern for leading a person from a
representational system which they are

already using, into another representational
system, either simultaneously or sequentially.

Pacing
The act of matching breathing, posture, movement,
voice tones and tempo with someone over
time, in order to develop rapport.

Paradigm
The aggregate of beliefs and values out of which a
culture, corporation or other group operates.

Parts
An imaginary division of an individual into
separate segments, each motivated by an
outcome the individual wants, and capable of
generating behaviour designed to obtain their
outcomes.

Pattern
Any sequence of features that repeats over time.

Perceptual filters (perceptual biases)
The socially and psychologically constructed bias
through which we filter our perceptions of the
world. Some perceptual filters remain the
same regardless of the state a person is in,
while others shift according to the state of the
perceiver. It is useful to be able to access an
extended range of perceptual filters, and
change filters, or build new filters at will. This

shifting of perceptual filters enables the user
to obtain a greater range and quality of
information about the world. The process of
perceptual filter flexibility is a major
component of a dynamic, balanced and
creative personality. According to John
Grinder "It is the Perceptual Filters that you
set just before you begin a class of activities
that are the difference that make the
difference ".

Perceptual Position
Any point of view taken by an individual at a given
time. The most commonly cited perceptual
positions are First Position, that of the
performer in their own body, Second Position,
that of the other, and Third Position, that of
the performer observing themselves and the
other from outside, usually equidistant from
First and Second. Other observer positions are
known as Meta Positions, and can be
anywhere, close or distant with a sight line to
that which is being observed.

Personal Ecology
Ensuring that choices made and activities
undertaken fit with one's beliefs and values in
the context of life, the future and other people.
We conduct this work in NLP within the
framework of personal ecology and personal
safety. By organising our selves or parts of self
with respect for ecology, it is possible to create

balance in the way we function to attain our outcomes and accommodate important values.

Personal evolution
The interaction of pattern, communication and relationship in our ongoing experience leading to new learning and new choices in one's behavioural flexibility.

Phonological Ambiguity
A word with different meaning and sometimes different spelling which sounds the same. eg. Heal and heel.

Physiology
Matters pertaining to the physical body and its use. The general posture and breathing of the individual is highly correlated with psychological state and cognitive processes. Note for yourself the difference in 'physiology' when contrasting a resourceful and unresourceful state eg. Excitement and interest compared to depression.

Posture, breathing and psychological state
The way we hold and move our physical selves in space has a direct affect on our psychological and emotional states as well as on our patterns of thinking. Learning additional movement patterns through the Feldenkrais method or the Alexander Technique enables greater flexibility of thinking and behaviour.

286

Conscious access to the posture and movement patterns which accompany resourceful states allows the individual to recreate those states at will.

Practical dream
Is a well formed vision represented in all the senses, placed in an appropriate position in the individual's future? This type of vision acts to set a direction and motivate an individual at both a conscious and unconscious level. To have the vision work effectively as a Practical Dream, it is essential to resolve any objections, especially those at the level of belief or identity.

Primary/Preferred System
The favoured representational system an individual uses in a particular situation or context. Used to be thought permanent but is now known to be too fleeting to label for use.

Present State
In NLP the present state is a description of the current cognitive and emotional state of an individual or group of individuals with reference to an outcome that they have selected. A Neuro-Linguistic Programmer may assist an individual or group to take an inventory of their Present State.

Presuppositions

Anything which is assumed, not stated, and can be
    inferred by referring to the source of the
    presupposition, be it an utterance, a sentence,
    a model, book, etc. For example, in the
    sentence, 'you have knocked it over again,' the
    presupposition is that you have knocked it
    over before. Cultural presuppositions are the
    unstated shared beliefs and understandings
    found in a culture. Personal presuppositions
    include beliefs and values which are important
    to an individual, although often outside
    conscious awareness. A quick way to elicit
    conscious awareness of anyone's
    presuppositions is to expose the person to a
    context in which their presuppositions are not
    shared by others.

Psychographic Space
The use of the space around an individual or group
    of individuals to influence the person/s placing
    and accessing of internal representations. A
    simple example is placing words for children
    to learn to spell, high up on the classroom
    walls so that visual accessing takes place. The
    art of shaping psychographic space can be
    more sophisticated than this example.

Psychological homeostasis
Mental stability.

Qualities

Emotional responses to any experience.

Quotes
A verbal communication pattern of giving
    suggestions / commands in the form of a quote
    from a character within a story. eg. ...and Jane
    turned to him and said 'you can make the most
    of this learning situation'.

Rapport
The engagement and holding of the unconscious,
    willing attention. When individual people or
    animals, or groups synchronize their
    behaviour, whether deliberately or
    unconsciously, they are said to be in rapport.
    Rapport can be established either by design, in
    which case one person matches another's
    behaviour, or it can arise spontaneously in
    response to a person's interest in the other. In
    this case the person matches the other
    unconsciously, through expressing their
    interest.

Reality
That which the individual believes to be so in the
    external world. A state in which a person's
    map is a close enough approximation to the
    external world for the individual's impact on
    the world to produce evidence of well formed
    outcomes.

Reality Check

The act of making external checks periodically to
ensure ecology is in place during internal
processing.

Reductionism

A pattern found within some scientific models of
the world, where everything is 'chunked down'
into smaller elements during analysis.

Reframing

Putting a different frame or perspective on one's
thoughts about a situation or example of
behaviour. Eg The half full/half empty glass. If
you want more, it is half empty; if you have
had enough, it is half full.

Reimprinting

The reorganisation and alteration of primary,
significant core representations from which
individuals derived limiting beliefs, and which
act as templates for behaviour within present
contexts.

Requisite Variety

A basic principle of cybernetics which states that in
any system of man or machines, the part of the
system with the greatest range of variability in
behaviour is the controlling element.

Representation

A picture, sound or feeling generated from within
to represent a concept, or a historical or future
event.

Representational Systems
The internal use of the senses for thinking; we can
represent the world in mental images, internal
sounds and feelings.

Resource
A piece of knowledge, an understanding about the
world, a belief, behaviour, a skill, a person or
an object, which contributes to the
achievement of an outcome.

Resourceful State
A psychological state that presupposes adequate
information, choices, flexibility in behaviour
and self reference in directing oneself in the
world.

Ritual
A stylised sequence of activity designed to anchor
and elicit a particular state or series of states
in the participants, with reference to the
leader's beliefs and values. Eg the use of
coloured pens, mind mapping and slow music
to elicit optimal learning states is a ritual
expression of the pattern of learning in all
three main representational systems.

Second Attention
Another name for the Unconscious mind.

Second nature
Any behaviour, capability or belief which has
    become automatic in a person's experience
    and is performed without conscious attention.

Second Order Change
Any change which takes place at a higher logical
    level than the problem state. This allows the
    change to affect the system, thereby rendering
    the erstwhile problem harmless, irrelevant or
    useful.

Second Position
The experience of taking a description through
    one's senses of another's psychological state,
    perception and viewpoint. A second position
    description can be obtained by matching the
    other's breathing, posture, movements, voice
    patterns and language patterns. It is a way of
    obtaining information of another's 'model of
    the world', and is useful as a precursor to
    bridging agreements and building
    understanding during negotiation. Although a
    second position description is by definition
    the individual's own representation of
    another's state, if done with care, it provides
    very accurate information about the other's
    processes, and can give clues to the subject
    matter they are considering.

Sensory Acuity

The ability to make refined distinctions in what one
sees, hears and feels. During a face to face
communication, practitioners of
Neuro-Linguistic Programming attend to
changes or shifts in the other's skin colour,
muscle tone, eye movements, breathing and
posture, and to voice tonal patterns, rhythm
and language used by the other. On the
telephone, auditory information alone is
available, and can be sufficient. This
information is used to calibrate the other's
internal state and cognitive processes. It is
considered in the world of NLP that sensory
acuity is a capability that can always be
improved.

Sensory based Description

A description in terms of what one can see, hear
and feel, either in the external world during an
experience, or in the describer's internal
experience.

Sensory Cues

The indicators we have through observation,
listening and touch, of a subject's ongoing
experience. These cues indicate that mental
processing is taking place; they do not identify
the content being processed.

Simulation Programming

293

Mental rehearsal of a future course of action with reference to a specific and expected situation, using internal representational systems to programme in the desired behaviours, capabilities and perceptual filters so that you can achieve the desired outcome in that situation. Also known as 'future pacing'.

State

This refers to the overall emotional physiological and psychological condition of an individual. It involves the beliefs, values, capabilities and behaviour within a context at a particular time. The concept of state can also be applied to a family, corporation or any social system.

State Choice

In the NLP model referred to as state control. The act of choosing deliberately to construct and inhabit a particular state in a given context, with the intention of achieving one's chosen outcome in that context.

Strategy

Any sequence of representations that leads to an outcome. The sequence and organization of representations (visual, auditory, kinaesthetic, olfactory and gustatory) which together comprise a thinking pattern. An effective strategy includes a representation of an outcome, employs feedback from the environment, and takes the minimum number of steps in a choreographed sequence to achieve the particular outcome of the strategy. Example of strategies explored in NLP include decision making, motivation, convincer, reality, learning and creativity strategies.

Submodalities
The sensory components within each of the modalities of the senses. Eg the sensory modality of visualisation is made up of components such as brightness, colour, hue, size and whether the image is framed of unframed etc. The auditory sensory modality has components such as stereo or mono, loudness, tempo and timbre quality etc.

Systemic thinking
Thinking in terms of pattern recognition, recursive manifestation of patterns, relationship between parts of a system, relationship between systems, patterns at similar and different logical levels, and patterns between logical levels.

Synaesthesia
When a signal is received or represented in one sense and is re- represented immediately in another representational system. The experience of sight/feeling, hearing/feeling etc. The test for a synaesthesia is to remove the first representation. If the second representation disappears at the sametime as

the first representation is removed, it is a synaesthesia.

Third Order Change
Any change in which the intervention is made two
   logical levels above that of the problem state. If
   first order is designed to be remedial and
   second order generative, then third order is
   evolutionary.

Third Position
This is an example of a Meta position. Third
   specifically is the observer of the relationship
   dance between the same person in first
   position, and the other, with whom they are
   interacting. Third is sometimes described as
   the observer, or director position. It watches,
   it has opinions about something which is
   occurring.

Through Time
A state in which the passage of time is perceived as
   being outside an individual, where they can
   see the past, present and future
   simultaneously. This is very good for planning,
   and activity which is enhanced by a
   dissociated state. This is the perception of the
   fixed duration appointment, and concepts of
   lateness, on time, lunch hours etc. Most
   western business uses a through time system.

Timelines
The internal subjective organization of individual
    perceptions of the passage of time. A timeline
    is the representation, usually by location in
    chronological order, of events from the past
    and projections of the future as images,
    sounds and feelings.

Time Orientation
Past, Present and Future: Individual preference for
    referencing one's perception of time. The past
    oriented person refers to history, enjoys
    nostalgia and relies on precedent to provide
    them with standards. Change has to be tried
    and tested before they will accept it. The
    present oriented person lives in the moment,
    likes instant gratification and does not make
    long term plans. The future oriented person
    plans, works and lives for the future,
    sometimes at the expense of ongoing
    experience. A combination of all three allows
    people to benefit from past experience, act in
    the present and plan for the future. They are
    also able to derive the most benefit from
    activities which relate to any one of the three
    orientations, e.g. a lawyer, who sails and
    invests in property.

Trance
Any state alteration from a pre-calibrated baseline
    state. Commonly used to refer to states

induced by someone using hypnotic
techniques, whether self or other.

Triple Description
Three different approaches to a single concept,
    preferably covering all three main
    representational systems, or three major
    perceptual positions. For modelling purposes,
    one can obtain a triple description by
    modelling three different experts in a
    particular field.

Unconscious mind (other than conscious mind)
Those parts of one's mental processes currently
    outside conscious awareness. Given that the
    conscious mind can only hold 7 + or - 2 chunks
    of information simultaneously, and the
    unconscious mind holds the bulk of one's
    information, the unconscious mind is worth
    cultivating.

Universal Quantifiers
Words denoting totality of quantity, eg all, every,
    none.

Unspecified Verbs
Verbs which apply to generic activity? |mp

Up-time State
In NLP a state where your attention is directed
    outward through your external senses with

minimum attention to inner subjective experience. Often it includes long distance and peripheral vision, an absence of internal dialogue, and optimal physiological posture and movement. An 'up time' state is particularly useful for activities requiring constant input of high quality information, such as presenting to groups.

Values
Those tenets upon which an individual's life is founded, made up of beliefs and ideals arising from the person's culture and family of origin, combined with their understanding of their own life experience. Normally classified in a hierarchy of importance. Eg stealing may be unacceptable normally, but with no money, and hungry dependents, one might steal for food and remain true to one's values.

Vestibular System
Originates from the Latin word vestibule, which means to contain or hold. The vestibular system is the sensory apparatus we use to orient our bodies in space, and to detect whole body movement. Its physical location is the semicircular canals in the ear, and the whole nervous system. As a representation system, the vestibular system is involved in the integration of information in the other representational systems, synaesthesia

patterns, and the ability to dissociate and associate. Use of the adjectives and verbs which predicate the vestibular system produces rapid induction of trance states in many subjects.

Vision
A representation of your desired future incorporating your most compelling Submodalities. It can be literal or metaphorical. Can also refer to an internal visual representation that the seer believes is likely to happen either to themselves or to others.

Visual
Pertaining to sight or the act of seeing.

Visualisation
The recall or construction in the visual modality of a picture, movie or visible scene. Refers to internal pictorial representation.

Well-formedness Conditions
Those conditions which, when met, provide for a strategy to be workable and ecological for its owner or those conditions which when met ensure that an outcome is well formed.

Well formed Outcome

An outcome that is stated in positive terms, has defined resources, is under the individual's control and respects positive by-products of the present state. see Present State.

The Twelve Questions

DR MIA MORGAN WHITE

Instructive Symbols

LOGO
TAKE TIME TO QUICK THINK / OR
CONTEMPLATE

When You see
ink wells PLEASE use this space to
take the time to Journal
in Here or enjoy the 12 QUESTIONS
Calendar. Remember see the ink well
write there if you want feel free
Plant Ink in those spaces

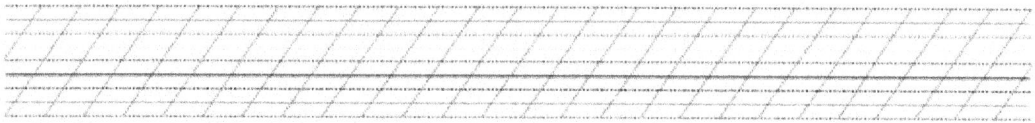

IN THE BEGINNING
WE WERE A SELF. THAT
SELF KNEW IT WAS A
SPARK OF GOD. PIECES
OF THE ALL THAT IS.
WE MUST KNOW OUR-
SELVES TO ENABLE US TO
FIND YOUR SELF. JOY-

DEVELOPED IN MY COACHING
PRACTICE
RECIPES FOR WELLNESS
DR. MIA MORGAN WHITE
SUBCONSCIOUS BARRIERS GONE
WAYS TO GET TO KNOW YOU
12 QUESTIONS

these grids are to show allotted times. Time to think, to partner, to discuss and respond. Give and get answers

Self time	Express time	Hypnosis	Balance
5 MIN	20 MIN	35 MIN	1600

ingredients that surfaced

Subconscious exercises

Please remember these are subconscious journeys. Questions created for my clients at $200 to 500 PER Session. To access the subconscious. Relax and have fun answering because you can't guess the right answer - because I am never asking you what you think, I am asking strange questions in a way to fix what you asked me to fix. Need fixed. Practitioners Never tell your clients the behind the scenes programming (that it is so they can stay relaxed). this is not a question of right and wrong but of being you.

results PROGRESSIVE DESTRUCTION OF PAINFUL MEMORIES

Dr. Mia Morgan White

THINK OF PAINTING THE ROSES RED
THE THINGS SOME THINK WHEN THE Y HAVE
POWER OVER YOUR LIFE CIRCUMSTANCE, THAT
INSTEAD OF EMPOWERING YOU ... THEY CAN PLAY
WITH YOUR ENERGY AND LIKE THE SAD LONELY
QUEEN IN ALICE THEY CAN MAKE YOU DO CRAZY
THINGS TO ENSURE YOUR SURVIVAL LIKE
MAKING YOU PAINTING WHITE ROSES RED.

IN every moment we are being programmed by friends,
TV family and others. We don't know this but that's
where our thoughts and behaviors come from... for
something, break bad programming, build a self you
love and figure out what you want to do, without other
people's voices.

12 QuestionsAwaken

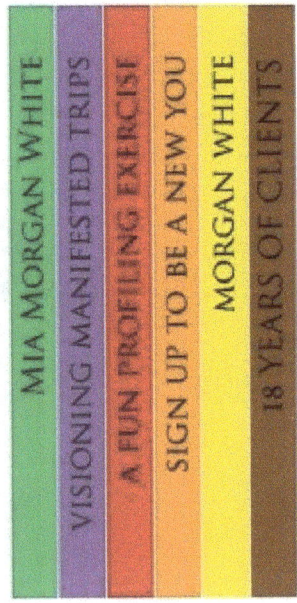

MIA MORGAN WHITE

VISIONING MANIFESTED TRIPS

A FUN PROFILING EXERCISE

SIGN UP TO BE A NEW YOU

MORGAN WHITE

18 YEARS OF CLIENTS

Previously Viewed

only the good stuff

We are going to do an exercise

directions
this is angel's bridge in rome

1. LEARNED FROM MEDITATION IN ROME LET EVERY BIRTH COUNT. - GROWTH EVERY BREATH BECAME EASY.

2. MEANWHILE, BACK IN THE STATES... AND I KEPT CHANGING ALL POSSIBLE. GROWTH SOMETIMES STARTLING, PAYS YOU.

3. WHEN WE REALIZE MUSIC HAS THE ABILITY TO DIVIDE GENRES AND MAKE SOULS WHOLE. ADJUST THE SPIRIT AND THE SOUL. - DON'T LET STRIFE DIVIDE YOU. KEEP WHOLENESS.

Close your eyes listen to me. If you are reading, record yourself on your phone and listen. Come to a training. Relax and see We have gone to a movie theatre and all the good things in our pasts and futures were filmed as a long reel Every Good Thing, in any order, smallest or chronological order. Take 10 minutes . Watch the Film, save the reel.

ANGELS BRIDGE

8 Minutes
Contempaltion

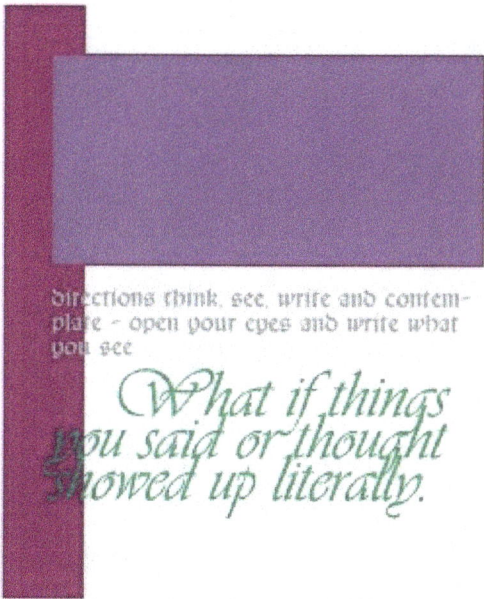

directions think, see, write and contemplate - open your eyes and write what you see

What if things you said or thought showed up literally.

TEMPLE EGYPT

If you went into time and space places what would you go get

directions
quick write or just contemplate when
doing these questions together.

If You had a Billion dollars what
would you do with your day.

Prep time	Answer time	Ready in	Section
07 MIN	22 MIN	02 MIN	11

ingredients

HEALING ANSWER. THE TRUE ANSWER IS ABOUT WHAT YOU
SHOULD DO FOR A BUSINESS / YOUR PURPOSE LIVING (RE-
VEALED ON SUBCONSCIOUS LEVEL 1QUEST CAN TELL ME 18
THINGS ABOUT YOU THAT ASKING 18 QUESTIONS YOU HAVE
CONTROL OVER WOULD NOT: WHAT YOU WOULD DO IN A DAY

I LEARNED A LOT FROM PEOPLE, WHO SAID: WHAT THEY
WOULD BUY PURCHASE (AS THIS WAS NOT THE QUESTION)
YOU SEE IT'S NOT JUST THE ANSWERS IT IS HOW YOU ANSWER.

SPECIAL NOTE: I TRIED LESS MONEY A MILLION WAS NOT
ENOUGH IN MY EARLY YEARS OF RESEACH TO FREE MOST
PEOPLES MINDS

IS ANSWERED BY

*If You had a Billion dollars
what would you do with your day.*

SUBCONSCIOUS IMPLANT

TRY HEART AND GOAL SEMINAR WORKSHOP
BECAUSE WE DON'T
   ALWAYS ADMIT TO OURSELVES OUR TRUE HEART

            FOR EXAMPLE THIS IS WHY I WENT TO PARIS.
MY SUBCONSCIOUS DEMANDED IT
            FEW PEOPLE SUPPORTED ME
IN GOING, THEY DOWN GRADED THE IDEA OF IT; AND SPOKE OF
THEIR FEARS FOR THEMSELVES.

NOT MANY PEOPLE SAY, WHAT THEY MEAN
WITHOUT WORRY. MORE PEOPLE SHOULD.

THE CHALLENGING /QUESTIONING OF
OUR NORMS IS THE PART OF THE PATH
TO ENLIGHTENMENT...THE SPACE
NARROWS AS YOU BEGIN TO TAKE
GROWTH MANY OTHERS MAY REJECT IT.

Using English, Art, Architecture and History

WE CREATE A SCIENTIFIC JOURNEY

OF THE HUMAN SUBCONSCIOUS, TIME ALLOWS US USING PHILOSOPHY,
ART, SCIENCE, CLASSIC LITERATURE BASED ON EDUCATION AND HOW PRO-
GRAMMING BEGAN, AND TRAVEL PHYSICAL AND SOUL; TRAVEL IN MIND
OR GO TO A PLACE AND MEDITATE.

I DEVELOPED A SYSTEM OR SEMINARS WHERE YOU HAD TO COME TO THE
SEMINAR TO GET THE BOOK, DEALING WITH A STALKER NO ONE WOULD
ARREST I CREATED SYSTEMS TO KEEP US ALL GOING. NO MATTER HOW
UNFAIR THE WORLD WAS BEING. NO MATTER WHAT HAPPENS DON'T GIVE
UP HOPE OR LISTEN TO OPINION OF VOYUERS OF HAPPINESS NEVER HAV-
ING ANY OF IT BUT TRYING TO ENSURE YOU DON'T LIVE YOUR DREAMS. AT
THAT TIME I DID A TALK CALLED DON'T GO CRAZY GO TO PARIS.

SEMINAR SETS STILL SOLD

When you picture yourself do you look like you in the mirror

A THEORY ON LOGIC -- DEVELOPED 18 THEORIES : THERE IS ALWAYS
MORE HAPPENING THAN MEETS THE EYE: YOU HAVE THE RIGHT TO EN-
JOY YOUR LIFE.

Peace

You can ask your self, or someone can ask you. Say your answers. Journal or Draw them

Mia's Recipe book

gaining Peace WITH Alternative PROCESSES Behavior

A BILLION DOLLARS

A FANTASY CREATURE

THE MUSICAL YOU

WHO YOU EMPOWER

INNATE INHERIENT HERO

FAITH AND JOY FILLING STATIONS

What is Right what people think of you or what you think of you?

12 *Questions Awaken*

MIA MORGAN WHITE
VISIONING MANIFESTED TRIPS
A FUN PROFILING EXERCISE
SIGN UP TO BE A NEW YOU
MORGAN WHITE
14 YEARS OF CLIENTS

What Super Power Would You Give A VIllain

Answer time	Discovery	Respond in	Serves
10 min	15 min	10 min	3 DAYS

directions
1. ANSWER.
2. ADD TO IT AS NEEDED.
3. LISTEN
4. DO
5. HAVE PERFECT BALANCE

UNDERSTANDING PROFILING

If you were stuck on an Island and could only listen to one Genre of Music for Life what would it be

WHAT WOULD IT BE NOW

Prep time	Response	Determination	Serves
15 min	20 min	25 min	7 years

Use Extra iN a TIME of Crisis your ingredients are:

1 just one genre (gives realistic tool set)

2 look for answer genre not song (is your client listening, were you clear, being a coach means listening)

3 note people who ask other people (tend to get wrong or group answers) that would be cheating

sheep run in groups LIONS run in packs!

Extra Notes about clients perception:

did they ask how the music would play

did they think of the musics affect on their joy

Because this will become part of their tool box --music that could keep them going

TOOL WILL BE DIFFERENT FOR EVERYONE

DIRECTIONS

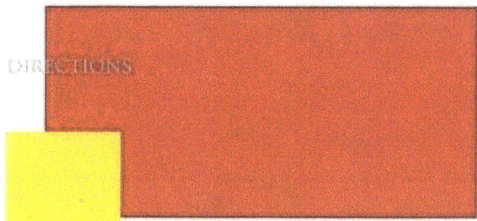

If You had a Billion dollars what would you do with your day.

Prep time	Answer time	Ready in	Section
07 MIN	22 MIN	02 MIN	11

ingredients

DIREC

What
if things
you said
or thought
showed up
literally.

If you could erase the entire history of two people's deeds who would it be

NUMBER

9

Can You Be A Vegetarian Who Hunts

Prep time	Ask time	Respond in	Serves
5 min	10 min	15 min	18

ingredients

directions

1. EXPLAIN YOUR RESPONSE WITHIN THE RESPOND TIME
2. an ANSWER I WOULD SAY NO BECAUSE_____

you can choose to do anything including stand up against
PAINTING THE ROSES RED
        THE THINGS THEY THINK THEY CAN MAKE YOU
        DO WHILE TRYING TO DRIVE YOU CRAZY

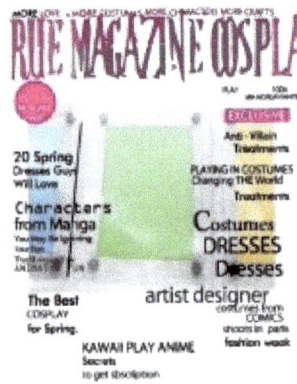

instant
feedback

Habits Of Healthy People

DIRECTIONS

1. Jump In
2. Go Through Doors
3. Don't Stay where you see it's wrong abusive or bad situation to you
4. Who were you - knowing who you are can save your life.
5. Many Tools Gained Here.
6. Offered as a Separate Training.

In Alice who are you.

Prep time	Cook time	Ready in	Serves
15 min	20 min	35 min	6

ingredients

Rabbit Holes
Crazy People
Injustice
Liars
Gossips
Corrupt Politicians
Love and Friendship
Growth

Dealing with Unjust situations, compassion fatigue. shows us gossips as Envy Spirits, Spiritual Growth from gifts of Moving Forward. Shows the results of the 7 deadly and the Strength of Self Confidence. Greed, Lust not thinking sloth as in the compared caucus race.

You have the ability to turn people into anything you want.

Name the People and what would they be

You Have Unlimited Time to Write Answers to This Question

in Alice Who ARe You

Does Your Name Suit You.

THE TWELVE QUESTIONS

WRITING MAKES THIS
QUESTION MOST
EFFECTIVE

What is

HOW TO PICK

your favorite question

What Is Your Fantasy Place to Be

Prep time	Aan time	Ready in	Sertive
15 MIN	20 MIN	35 MIN	12

instant changing

DID YOU LIMIT YOURSELF BY SPACE AND TIME

PLANNING A NEW YOU

A REAL WORLD OR SCI FI

THESE LIMITS TELL ME A LOT

PARIS WHEN I WENT TO PARIS NO BODY BELIEVED IN ME NOT FOR ONE OF THE 46 TRIPS. WHAT IF I HADN'T GONE BASED ON SOMEBODY ELSE'S BELIEF IN MY.

LIST PLACES YOU KNOW YOU COULD LIVE

WERE YOU A PERSON OR OBJECT

Is THERE
Something
Buried Under
The Circus

SHOWING

INSIGHTS

IN YOUR FANTASY WHERE IS YOUR PERFECT
PLACE.

BEAWARE THESE ANSWERS EXPOSES MORE ABOUT
FEELINGS ABOUT WHERE YOU ARE

Egypt

Health AND▷

Science

NEXT TITLE HE SAID LET THERE
BE LIGHT AND WE WERE

Dr Mia Morgan White

POWER MIND

Subconscious Secrets HOW to PROTECT YOUR HAPPINESS. an Enhanced Book: The Truth People Don't Usually Want to Tell You about Energy Subconscious and Conscious Action, Conscious Mind Power